*Perceptual-Motor Efficiency
in Children*

Perceptual-Motor

The Measurement and

BRYANT J. CRATTY, Ed.D.

Associate Professor and Director, Perceptual-Motor Learning Laboratory, Department of Physical Education, University of California, Los Angeles

Efficiency in Children

Improvement of Movement Attributes

SISTER MARGARET MARY MARTIN, M.A., M.S.
Associate Professor and Chairman, Department of Physical Education, Alverno College, Milwaukee, Wisconsin

Lea & Febiger   Philadelphia, 1969

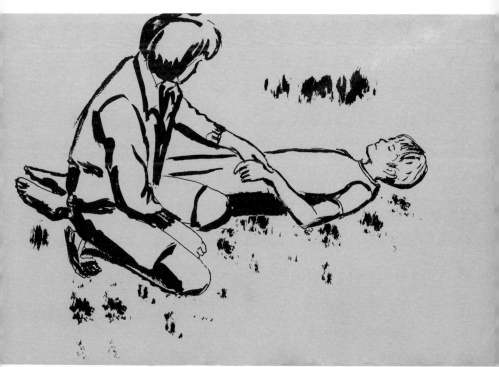

Health Education, Physical Education, and Recreation Series

RUTH ABERNATHY, Ph.D., EDITORIAL ADVISER
Chairman, Department for Women, School of Physical and Health Education, University of Washington, Seattle, Washington, 98105.

to the memory of Robert F. Kennedy

Foreword

Man's ability to make use of symbols is perhaps the most important attribute which distinguishes him from other animals. This ability is obviously a direct result of what we call intelligence. Therefore, it comes as no surprise that the child who has difficulty utilizing the symbols of his culture presents a major problem to his parents and his teachers and finds himself handicapped in competition with his peers. He has a learning disability. He is an *exceptional child.*

Simple as this descriptive phrase may sound, it encompasses a multitude of children with a multitude of symptoms springing from a multitude of causes. Variously described as minimally brain damaged, motor impaired, emotionally disturbed, perceptually disabled, dyslexic, neurologically disorganized, dysgraphic, aphasic, autistic, to name but a few, they have one thing in common; a significant educational discrepancy between their *apparent* capacity for language behavior and their *actual* functional language level. Of interest to pediatrician and neurologist, educator and psychologist, it is small wonder that a diversity of thought and theory now provides a confusing picture for parents and teachers who must deal daily with the problem in fact.

To the educator, the problems can be broadly divided into three major categories, reading disorders (dyslexia), verbal communication or language disorders, and visual-motor or perceptual-motor integration problems. In fact, more often than not, there is general overlapping among these groupings. Faced with the mammoth problem of trying to teach these children—who may represent as high as 10 to 15 per cent (Barsch puts the figure at 30 per cent) of their students—educators have grasped at almost any theoretical straw offered as the magic key to free the potential locked behind these mysterious barriers to normal cerebral functioning. Among the most popular of these currently are remedial systems based largely on the relationship of body movement to the learning process.

It has been said that little can be done to stop an idea whose time has come. Such seems to be the case in the use of movement as a therapeutic agent for the exceptional child. Such an idea, particularly when filling what has essentially been a void, can gather hurricane force that makes difficult any serious or scientific consideration of its validity. The work of analysis becomes doubly difficult when it involves subjects as elusive as intelligence and learning backed by the emotional force of a problem affecting millions of children. Such a situation draws both scientist and charlatan into its maelstrom with the predictable outpouring of considerable "flotsam" and few pearls. For the parent or teacher it often becomes difficult to distinguish between the good, the bad, and the indifferent. Many physicians and educators, Cratty and Martin point out, as a result of the recent "evangelical-like preoccupation with movement as a panacea for a variety of childhood difficulties," have become skeptical that any of these movements (pun intended) results in any appreciable benefit to the child's learning ability. For this reason alone, this book is particularly timely.

Not surprisingly, worried parents eagerly reading in the popular press of promised miracles offered the brain-damaged child by enthusiastic proponents of various neuro-motor training programs are confused and angered when they find little support for these particular approaches from their child's physician or teacher. Or, having embarked on such strenuous and time-consuming motor and sensory regimens, often at great personal and financial cost, find little improvement and no miracles. The intellect wrapped within the enigma of the brain has failed to come forth at the beckoning of sensory stimuli coming from muscles and joints passively moved in the hands of well-meaning others. Similarly disappointing results can be anticipated in those programs teaching splinter motor skills—whether it be learning to creep or to bounce on a trampoline—unless, as clearly brought out in this text, the child is encouraged to think about what he is doing and is involved in a way which encourages the process of decision-making.

Few serious scientists in recent years have been more productive in both analytic and experimental explorations of the relationships between mental and motor functioning in the exceptional child than Professor Cratty. His "Movement Behavior and Motor Learning" (1964) analyzed the contributions of such diverse fields as psychology, anthropology, and engineering to problems of concern to physical educators and provided a basic text on the perceptual-motor foundations of physical education. In "Social Dimensions of Physical Activity" (1967) he summarized the pertinent research on the possible influence of selected social variables upon human movement, and provided a speculative base for future research on "—the social dimensions of physical activity—and the physical dimensions of social activity." His most recent publication, "Perceptual-Motor Behavior and the Educational Process," (1969) explored with an admirable objectivity some of the recent "movement panaceas," particularly in their relationship to special education. His research publications include a wide spectrum of studies involving movement and learning in normal populations, the mentally retarded, and the blind.

The present volume directed primarily at educators and parents, is written with cool objectivity, avoiding the pseudo-scientific jargon and Messianic fervor characteristic of some similarly directed writings. Cratty and Martin present a brief but excellent review of the current literature bearing on the relationship of body movement to learning and intelligence. Both parent and professional will profit from their candid analysis in Chapter 2. They find little support for the assumption that "motor learning is the basis of all learning." The pitfalls in many of the correlative studies purporting to show increased IQ's as a result of increased physical fitness or skills are pointed out. They similarly question the studies supporting the Doman-Delacato program of movement education and point out its proponents' reluctance to subject their methods to experimental verification. The concentration on cerebral dominance or the problem of cross-dominance as an important etiology factor in children with learning problems is appropriately minimized. While concluding that ''Dr. Kephart has made a significant contribution to the understanding and remediation of some of the perceptual-motor difficulties of the neurologically impaired—,'' they raise questions about some of his theoretical framework.

The program for development of perceptual-motor efficiency as presented in this text would appear to be soundly based on principles of child development. The importance of motivating children to learn, a point so often overlooked by both parent and teacher, is clearly stressed. While providing a better understanding to parents on the use of movement activities as an aid to learning in children, the authors point out that programs utilizing these techniques should be under the direction of trained personnel who understand the rationale underlying the procedures. Furthermore, they point out, no child should be entered into such a program without ''—a thorough and comprehensive evaluation of the emotional, social, educational, perceptual, and motor functioning of the child.'' If these basic guide lines of the authors are understood and followed, much of the previous criticism from pediatricians and educators can be avoided.

Paul H. Pearson, M.D., M.P.H.
Meyer Professor of Child Health
Director, Meyer Children's Rehabilitation Institute
University of Nebraska College of Medicine
Omaha, Nebraska

Preface

In addition to the subtle components of the child's personality traditionally dealt with in educational literature, an increasing amount of attention is being paid to his more obvious attributes. The general movement behavior and specific motor skills of children in elementary schools have begun to come in for closer inspection for several reasons. (*a*). Theories have emerged which suggest that movement may aid learning in a general way; (*b*). some educators have become aware that emotional problems may be caused by motor ineptitudes evidenced in the classroom and on the playground; (*c*). educators and parents have begun to realize that they may institute significant changes in the motor skill of children which will, at times, be reflected in positive changes in the manner in which the child functions socially; (*d*). since many of the childhood diseases have either been eliminated or controlled, the less obvious problems of children (moderate "clumsiness") have been brought to the attention of parents by perceptive physicians.

This increased concern for motor functioning, however, has at times been accompanied by an evangelical-like pre-occupation with movement as a panacea for a variety of childhood difficulties. As with any type of overaction, whether in the educational, social, or political arena, the evidences of a subsequent "backlash" are beginning to emerge. Some educators are beginning to evidence skepticism and rejection of any kind of perceptual-motor, sensory-motor, motor-sensory, etc., training.

Either viewpoint, it is believed, tends not to do justice to the manner in which motor activity can contribute to the total development of the child. We do not feel that efficient movement is the imperative base from which all cognitive, perceptual, auditory, emotional, and social attributes must necessarily spring. At the same time, it is believed that motor activities may be employed more effectively as an important type of teaching tool in programs of elementary education. It has been attempted, within the pages of this book, to delineate just how this "movement tool" may be more highly polished. The initial chapters contain critical discussions of the currently available literature linking movement with perceptual and intellectual skills. The final portions of the text contain rationale as well as practices helpful to classroom teachers, curriculum supervisors, administrators, and parents.

Within the text are contained norms which should be referred to by individuals purporting to identify and to help the inept.

If the book serves the purpose of making teachers and administrators sensitive to the 10 per cent of their classroom of "normal" children who tend to exhibit perceptual-motor difficulties, our primary objective will be realized.

At times, needed averages were obtained utilizing the research staff within our laboratory at the University of California at Los Angeles. Information dealing with games-choice, drawing behavior, gross-motor attributes, as well as self-concept was obtained in this way.

It is hoped that the material in the book will be of interest and help to individuals with a diversity of backgrounds. Classroom teachers and parents should be aided by the techniques contained in Chapters 5, 6, 7, and 9. It is hoped, however, that practitioners will not ignore the rationale for their practices contained in some of the earlier chapters. Knowing *why* one is doing things with children is believed more productive than simply carrying out operations.

Research scholars should be interested in the review of the literature, containing discussions of current theories and reasonably comprehensive bibliography. Curriculum supervisors, school psychologists, and others concerned with evaluation and assessment should be aided by the norms contained in Chapters 3 and 6. These averages may be utilized to formulate screening devices or to obtain more exact measures of children's performance.

We are indebted to numerous individuals who aided in the production of the book, and in the collection of data contributing to its content. Mr. Thomas Durkin, Mr. John Kaufman, and Mr. Jeffrey Drucker tested children within our clinic program at the University of California at Los Angeles and gained data upon which much of the information contained in the text is based. Mrs. Jane Durkin, Miss Trish Spradlin and Mr. Drucker aided in the reduction of data and in the preparation of the Appendix and references. Mrs. Kathleen Fujimoto employed her formidable typing and editorial skills in the production of the final manuscript.

Mr. Barry Preiss, Miss Cherie Ritchie, and Mrs. Janet Zeller collected data resulting in norms for drawing behavior and gross-motor ability contained in Chapters 3 and 6 Mr. Martin Wilner, with the cooperation of Mr. Jack Macey, Principal in the Montebello School District in Los Angeles County, obtained data which resulted in averages for the games-choice test.

It is believed that the manuscript is enhanced immeasureably by the technically and artistically well-executed drawings. Our thanks for this contribution are extended to our illustrator, Miss Lynn Vander Velde.

The material in the text is based upon data collected from over 2,000 children during the past three years taking part in a dozen research studies. To them also gratitude is extended.

Dr. Madeline Hunter, Principal of the University of California at Los Angeles' University Elementary School and her staff cooperated with us by permitting her students to be tested. The norms for figure drawing, and gross-motor tests are based upon their scores. We would like to thank Dr. Hunter and her staff for their hospitality during the past two years.

We are further indebted to Paul Pearson, M.D., Professor of Child Health, University of Nebraska College of Medicine, whose helpful review of the manuscript and contribution of the Foreword are both valuable contributions. Finally, the authors are grateful to the parents and children within the clinic program at the University of California at Los Angeles for tolerating their searchings, testings, and inconsistencies during the past eight years.

BRYANT J. CRATTY
SISTER MARGARET MARY MARTIN

Los Angeles, California
Milwaukee, Wisconsin

Contents

1

Introduction

The attention of educators has focused to an increasing degree upon the movement attributes of children. Several contributing factors to this interest are: (*a*) the emergence of well publicized theories which suggest that aiding a child to move better will remediate other educational deficiencies; (*b*) the tasks stemming from these theories are relatively easy to execute and to understand; (*c*) the growing awareness among educators that the obvious things some children cannot do well may contribute directly or subtly to their total well-being.

At times, however, the emphasis placed by some on motor activities has confused educators and parents. Some theoreticians, for example, have suggested that engaging in relatively simple motor tasks will remediate a variety of perceptual, sensory, and cognitive deficits.

While we do not take such an expansive view, it is believed that movement activities should be exploited more fully as educational tools. In the chapters which follow we have attempted to delineate in just what ways the participation in and improvement of motor skills may contribute to the total development of the maturing child.

Available evidence suggests that children participating in programs of perceptual-motor education improve only those attributes trained for, [10, 2, 11] and nothing more. Motor activity will aid a child to think to the extent to which he is encouraged to think about his movements. Programs utilizing stylistic, unmotivated action, in which children move about as directed by an instructor, have failed to modify the wide variety of attributes they claim to effect. [10, 8]

It is essential, however, that perceptual-motor deficits be identified as early as possible in the life of a child. At times the obstetrician is able to do this at birth, particularly if the child evidences obvious problems. By the end of the first year, the competent pediatric neurologist can often identify a child with minimal or moderate problems of motor control. Cognizant of the problems, these medical experts are many times able to plan a remedial program.

Unfortunately, circumstances often tend to prevent this early identification of subtle motor deficits in many children, and valuable time is lost. During these first months of life, a child is observed primarily by his parents, and he is often not under the prolonged observation of experts in the medical field and the behavioral

2

sciences. Usually, it is after the child manifests very obvious perceptual-motor deficits later in life that he is placed under the scrutiny of medical experts.

While it is reasonable to expect parents to become suspicious of certain movement abnormalities, all too frequently they are distracted from them by other components of their child's behavior. For example, an easily elicited smile from a child may blunt the parents' awareness of a delay in walking. Furthermore, many parents are unaware of stages in perceptual-motor behavior through which a child normally passes as he develops. Therefore, during the important pre-school years, subtle motor deficits may progressively worsen.

However, when a child is placed with his peer group in kindergarten or first grade, his ineptitude usually becomes obvious to his teacher. At this time, his parents may learn from his teacher that he is "clumsy", because he handles scissors poorly, his drawings are inaccurate, or perhaps because he has difficulty when attempting to catch a ball. Only then do many parents fully realize the difficulties their child is having when attempting to move accurately in the classroom and on the playground.

There are times, however, when a teacher may lack insight in a particular child's problem or perhaps because she has too many children in her classroom. The child with minor perceptual-motor problems, finishing last in drawing and writing tasks will begin to experience feelings of failure and may receive admonitions from the teacher for his failure to complete a job requiring accurate hand movements within the allotted time. This punishment may begin to spawn a "syndrome of failure" which may lower his aspiration level and may result in his withdrawal from activities in which he must make accurate movements, thus further "blunting" his movement attributes.

In his book, *Stability and Change in Human Characteristics,* Benjamin Bloom has summarized a number of studies in which attributes within populations of children and adults have been measured for successive years.[1] Of the several axioms Bloom derived from this survey, one has an important implication for the remediation of perceptual-motor problems. According to Bloom, to elicit the greatest possible change in an attribute, modification should be attempted when the attribute is normally in a state of greatest flux. It is apparent from the available clinical and experimental evidence that the greatest amount of perceptual-motor change occurs in children before the age of seven years. It is therefore imperative that children with perceptual-motor deficits be identified as soon as possible, and that efforts be made during these early years of life to aid them to improve their ability to move accurately.

A research clinical program for children with moderate perceptual-motor problems has been operative for several years at the University of California at Los Angeles. During this period of time, 600 children have been evaluated and selected for inclusion in the program. In an effort to change their perceptual-motor behavior, children with similar problems were assigned to small groups, and under the direction of trained instructors, they participated in activities designed to alleviate their motor deficits.

During these years, numerous assessment devices have been applied, some of which were discarded for better measures. Since 1966, the evaluation procedures have been stabilized. Most of the tests in the present battery have been administered to normal populations of children in an effort to make meaningful analyses of the various sub-populations of children in the clinical setting described.

Several research studies have been carried out during this period. Some have compared pre- and post-testing results within the population of children dealt with directly. Other studies were made in which the attributes of indigenous populations were compared with those of other children. The results of some of these investigations are reported in the chapters which follow.

After surveying available literature, analyzing data collected from within the program, and subjectively observing the effects of various methodologies upon the attributes measures, we have arrived at several conclusions.

1. Programs of perceptual-motor education are likely to elicit change in those attributes trained for. [11, 10] Attributes such as: balance, left-right discrimination of body parts, hand-eye coordination, agility, and sports skills will change in varying degrees in children with moderate to mild deficits. More change is more likely to occur in children with mild deficits than in those with more pronounced problems and in younger than in older children.

2. Unless the principles for the transfer of learning are applied, however, it is unlikely that such training will result in marked changes in the academic success of educationally handicapped children.

3. A promising direction of future research in perceptual-motor education involves a closer look at individual differences in learning potentials, strategies, physiques, personality traits, and perceptual-motor attributes which contribute in subtle and complex ways to the learning success of individual children. [5]

For example, improvement in the learning abilities of children from higher income groups may come about by engaging in motor activities, because they have lacked this type of experience. On the other hand, the economically deprived child with learning difficulties, having had a wide variety of play experiences, may need more verbal-linguistic experiences to lay a foundation for his success in school.

4. Not all children entering school have a need for special "doses" of perceptual-motor education to help them to learn. For some children, a comprehensive physical education program is sufficient. It is important, however, that school administrators identify children with perceptual-motor deficits as soon as possible, so they can be placed in remedial programs.

5. The laboratory demonstration program conducted by us has, as its ultimate aim, the establishment of special remedial programs in elementary schools in which children with movement problems may obtain special help. Such programs should concentrate on both fine and gross motor skill. Therefore, practice should include tasks leading toward, and directly related to, skills which are essential to a child's classroom and playground success.

6. The worth of new components of the total educational program encompassing movement activity should continue to be evaluated, as far as possible, by reference to research data which describe in precise terms just what behavioral changes in children may be elicited through what specific practices.

7. Special aid for children with movement difficulties is justified for several reasons. A child with hand-eye coordination problems will often be unable to easily

transcribe his thoughts on paper. This ineptitude frequently results in a negative attitude toward starting an assignment which he knows he will be unable to complete.

A child with problems of large muscle control will usually be less acceptable to his peers as he engages in games. There is evidence to support the view that an optimum amount of social acceptance is associated with academic success. If a child's social status within a class is low, it is likely his academic efforts will suffer.[12]

It is almost inevitable that a child with movement problems will suffer from concomitent problems involving emotional adjustment. To reduce these adjustment problems professionals should institute remediation at the subtle level, as well as attempting to change the more obvious facets of his behavior, things he cannot do well and about which he harbors bad feelings.

8. While some children with movement problems withdraw from activity, other children evidence the apparent inability to stop moving! Motor activities, correctly applied, may exert a quieting influence on the over-aroused child.

9. Games and game-like problem-solving situations have proved to be a motivating and effective way of instilling some classroom competencies into some children. Serial memory ability in letter and number problems, as well as verbal and arithmetic skills have improved in naturally active boys and girls, as well as in groups of atypical children.[3, 6]

Movement, *per se,* is not the solution to all learning problems. Some children are intellectually superior, yet they are physically handicapped to the extent that movement is impossible for them. On the other hand some children are well coordinated, yet evidence severe learning problems.

An overview of the clinical experiences afforded by the problems described, and supported by recently published research studies, however, lead us to believe that movement experiences which improve the perceptual-motor capacities of children will play an increasingly important role in education.

The purpose of this book is to reach two important groups of people, parents and educators, both of whom have the opportunity and the need to identify the child having slight to moderate perceptual-motor problems. Guidelines are presented to help parents recognize certain deficits during the vital early years when their child is under their supervision. It is hoped that the text will aid school administrators, curriculum specialists, and classroom teachers select assessment tools for surveying the population of children for whom they are responsible. To predict and to remediate motor problems at an early age is far more beneficial to the child than to recommend him to remedial programs after he has been subjected to frustrations and failures in the classroom, exclusion from normal play experiences, and social rejection by his peers on the playground.

REFERENCES

1. Bloom, Benjamin S.: *Stability and Change in Human Characteristics,* New York, John Wiley & Sons, Inc., 1964.
2. Brown, Roscoe C.: "The Effect of a Perceptual-Motor Education Program on Percep-

tual-Motor Skills and Reading Readiness," Speech Presented at Research Section, AAHPER Convention, St. Louis, Missouri, April 1, 1968.

3. Cratty, Bryant J.: *Learning Games, 50 Games for Atypical Children,* Freeport, New York, Educational Activities Inc., 1968.

4. Delacato, Carl, H.: *The Treatment and Prevention of Reading Problems,* Springfield, Charles C Thomas, 1959.

5. Gagne, Robert M. (Ed.): *Learning and Individual Differences,* Columbus, Ohio, Charles E. Merrill Books, Inc., 1967.

6. Humphrey, J. H.: *Child Learning Through Elementary School Physical Education,* Dubuque, Iowa, Wm. C. Brown Co., 1966.

7. Kershner, John R.: "Doman-Delacato"s Theory of Neurological Organization Applied With Retarded Children, *Except. Child.; 32,* 441–450, 1967.

8. LaPray, M. and Ross, R.: "Auditory and Visual-Perceptual Training," in *Vistas In Reading,* Ed. J. Allen Figural, International Reading Association Conference Proceedings, XI, 530–32, 1966.

9. Leighton, J. M., Cupp, A., Prince, D., Philabeaum, G., and McLarren, L.: "The Effect of a Physical Fitness Development Program on Self-Concept, Mental Age, and Job Proficiency in the Mentally Retarded," *J. Phsyiol. & Ment. Rehab.: 20,* 4-11, 1966.

10. Robbins, Melvyn, P.: "A Study of the Validity of Delacato's Theory of Neurological Organization," *Except. Child: 32,* 617-523, April 17, 1966.

11. Solomon, A. and Prangle, R.: "Demonstrations of Physical Fitness Improvement in the EMR," *Except. Child. 33:* 177–181, Nov. 1967.

12. Weatherford, R. S. and Horrocks, J.: "Peer Acceptance and Over and Under Achievement in School, *J. Psychol., 66,* 215–220, 1967.

2

Perception, Motion, and Thought: A Review of the Literature

Experimental data are available which describe relationships between movement and cognition and between movement and perception. Frequently children with learning problems will evidence lip movement when they are trying to think through a problem of some sort. On the other hand, mental activity, especially if it is intense, is sometimes accompanied by an increase in general muscular tension.[33] In populations of children in which brain damage has resulted in movement deficiencies, a larger percentage of these children will evidence concomitant intellectual deficits than will be found among populations of normal children. Conversely, in populations of children identified as having learning problems, many will manifest clumsy motor behavior in big muscle activities and/or they will have difficulty with writing skills and other fine motor skills.

It is difficult, however, to locate definitive research studies which delineate the manner in which motor activity may *cause some change* in another component of a child's perceptual or intellectual makeup. In fact, it is often hard to find evidence which supports the fact that *motor* education improves in a general way the *motor* attributes of a given child or population of children! A child with learning difficulties is likely to have motor problems because a third variable, *i.e.,* some type of neurological impairment may affect both his mental and motor functioning. However, motor problems are often seen in children who have been labeled as intellectually gifted; while children with severe movement deficits (or among populations of armless children) have been found who can achieve superior scores in tests of I.Q.[1,40]

A survey of the literature is further complicated by the fact that sound research studies from the laboratories of competent scholars are often difficult for a teacher or administrator in a remote school district to obtain, if indeed their duties leave them time to examine this type of literature. In addition, these studies are often caged in technical language and sprinkled with statistics both of which are difficult for the uninitiated to interpret.

On the other hand, pronouncements which are often easier to obtain, but less scholarly in their approach, dealing with relationships between perception and motion and between thought and movement are liberally represented in the popular press. This latter type of publication may secure the attention of anxious parents and mislead them. Parental pressure may then be exerted upon school personnel to try the latest movement panacea whose favorable outcomes have been proclaimed in the latest issues of some popular magazine.

This chapter will attempt to synthesize available literature and to interpret claims and statements which infer causal relationships between perception, cognition, and motion. We believe it is important to clarify the role of motor activity in education and on the personality development of the child. A brief survey of the role of visual training, which often accompanies education in motor activities, is also undertaken. An evaluation will be made of some of the broad statements involving movement as an educational tool. The sense and nonsense permeating such statements as . . . "Motor is the basis for all learning" . . . and "Movement will aid perceptual development" . . . will be explored. Data exploring various causal relationships between motor activity and reading readiness will be discussed.

We believe that motor activity has an important place within the educational program of all children, and certainly within programs for atypical children. But if claims for movement are not carefully assessed, and if reasonable outcomes for movement education are not predicted, the actual value of improved perceptual-motor functioning may never be realized.

MOVEMENT AND THE INTELLECT

Studies in which motor activity has been linked to cognitive function are of three primary types. (*a*). Correlative studies in which statistical comparisons are made between mental, academic, perceptual, and motor scores; (*b*). experimental studies in which programs of perceptual-motor education are evaluated by the extent to which they change other attributes; (*c*). and studies of the development of perceptual-motor capacities in infants.

Correlative Studies. Correlative studies have been conducted over the years and their findings usually point to positive but non-significant relationships between scores obtained on motor tasks and measures of I.Q.[3, 7, 12, 86] At times, the authors of these investigations have claimed that even these low correlations infer that there is a motor base to the intellect or that participation in physical acts will somehow improve intelligence.[51]

It must be kept in mind that a correlation does not necessarily prove causality, and when one obtains a correlation between a motor task score and an intelligence score, it may suggest that some degree of thought has contributed to the performance of the motor act.

For example, studies of atypical children have been carried out in which a score in a direct and *simple* motor act (*e.g.,* jump, reach) was contrasted to I.Q. with no appreciable relationship discernible. However, when the score of a more complex four-count task (squat-thrust to a push-up position, return to a squat and rise) was compared to that from an I.Q. test, a moderate relationship emerged.[26] It is obvious that the second motor act involved required the same ability to remember a series of directions as do some items in intelligence tests.

Ismail and Gruber,[51] in a recent monograph, obtained small correlations between I.Q. measures and motor tasks in which five items of information had to be remembered by the performing child (*i.e.,* "Hop twice on your left foot, then hop twice on your right without hesitation."). It was only after low achieving children were utilized as subjects that even these slight correlations were uncovered (.3 and .4 indicates a common variance of only from 9 to 16 per cent).

Little justification for the statement that motor learning is the basis of all learning or that movement is the basis of the intellect can be gained from correlative studies of this nature, if one accepts the rationale upon which the intellectual measures and motor performance measures are based.

When claims are made that a relationship exists between motor performance and intelligence, a careful delineation must be made of the exact *complexity* of the motor tasks used in the comparison. If a population of normal children is used, and one begins contrasting motor tasks of increasing complexity with their intelligence scores, increasingly higher correlations result. These findings suggest that movement, *per se,* is not the base from which *all* human attributes emerge. Rather they suggest simply that the performance of many motor tasks is dependent to some degree upon thought. It may be possible, however, to improve a child's thought processes by encouraging and stimulating the child to think about his movements.

Muska Mosston supports this conclusion in his theory of a spectrum of teaching styles.[69] Taking a position similar to that advanced by several scholars interested in cognitive processes, Mosston holds that true learning takes place only if the child has some control over decisions permeating the learning environment. He contends that a stimulus-response type of learning is not appropriate for the optimum development of the human intellect.

Mosston suggests that a gradual transfer of decision-making from the instructor to the learner should be paced according to the child's ability to assume the responsiblility for making the decision. According to him, teachers should proceed from situations in which the teacher gives commands governing the behavior of the learner to situations in which the learner is permitted to make decisions about modifying the task. Later, when the teacher believes the child is capable of doing it, he is allowed to make those decisions which the teacher usually reserves for himself, *i.e.,* evaluation and devising activities to meet specified goals.

Unfortunately, this methodology, while sometimes used in classrooms, has not received extensive attention by experimentalists. However, one study carried out on normal children, in which behaviors elicited by the traditional command-teaching were compared to those elicited by this problem-solving approach, indicated that the students subjected to the latter methodology evidenced more flexible response patterns which accommodated to the changing complexities of game strategies. Students taught only skill specifics learned these skills more exactly and quickly than the others, but they lacked the flexibility of response.[100]

It would appear, however, that the methodology espoused by Mosston has important implications for the education of children through movement. Activities of this nature are explored in Chapter 11.

Causal Studies. Another type of evidence, important to consider in this context, has arisen from studies made to determine the causative effects of a physical activity program on measures of intelligence. Some of these have examined the effects of the structured movement programs such as that espoused by Doman-Delacato.[59] Other studies have combined simple locomotor tasks with visual training and "reflex-like" patterning movements.[9,61] Additional research has explored the influence of traditional physical education programs on scores of academic achievement and intelligence.[62,71,17,70]

At times, the methodologies and conclusions arising from this research may be questioned. One study, for example, excluded children-subjects from the study if observant teachers thought the I.Q. scores obtained were invalid.[51] Another research study concluded that one of the movement theories was tenable, even though more improvement was elicited in a wide variety of perceptual-motor tasks on the part of the *control group* [59] than in his experimental group. Another experimenter utilized only 8 subjects in his experimental group.[17]

In general, the findings of these investigations point to the need for delineating more precisely the nature of the population to whom motor activities are applied and for more control of the variables which might have influenced changes. Identification of intervening variables such as improved self-concept or increased physical stamina are necessary because they may affect the learning capabilities of a child.

Scholars, concerned with the emerging concept of individual differences in learning, should be heeded by researchers interested in describing the possible influence of motor activity upon intellectual potential and academic achievement of children.[34] For example, in 1958, James Oliver found that he could significantly improve (by 25 per cent) the I.Q.'s of educable retardates by subjecting them to an extra three hours a day of physical activity in which they learned recreational skills and participated in fitness activities. Oliver speculated that the improvement elicited stemmed from a heigthened motivational state and an improved self-concept.[71]

Corder, perhaps encouraged by Oliver's work, similarly found that improvement in I.Q. was elicited by a program of physical education. In this second study, a group was inserted which interacted socially with the experimenter, as well as one which received no attention, together with an experimental "physical education" group to control for the well-known "Hawthorn Effect" (the influence of personal attention and experimenter rapport upon the measures of behavioral change obtained.)[17]

A more definitive investigation completed by Solomon and Prangle found that improvement in a *retardate* population subjected to a special physical education program was obtained only in motor ability, with I.Q. and other measures of school achievement remaining unaffected.[93]

These conflicting findings between Oliver's and Solomon and Prangle's studies probably arise from a failure to delineate the personality trait structures, learning strategies, and similar factors within the groups studied. Oliver's subjects may have suffered from a lack of self-confidence when performing motor activities and when their skill improved, they "blossomed"; whereas the group tested by Solomon and Prangle may have contained self-confident children who felt comfortable in motor activities before he began experimenting with them.

Furthermore, it must be remembered that many things happen to experimental subjects before the researcher enters their lives, to insert, usually for a brief period of time, something which it is hoped will change them in some way. It is this fact which influences the type of findings usually obtained in studies of transfer of training when normal subjects are utilized; the transfer to the second activity has usually occurred in the subjects' lives long before they have been exposed to the experimental conditions for a few minutes a day.

A review of the literature makes it apparent that at least average acceptance by a child's peers is necessary before he can be expected to achieve academically.[99] If a child is rejected socially, it is likely that his self-concept will suffer, and this in turn will be reflected in poor classroom work. This does not mean that raising a child's status in his social group will inevitably improve academic achievement because there is research that shows just the opposite to be true. However, research demonstrates that children who are very popular within their social group may not perform well academically since they are too distracted with their social activities to study![99]

The findings of studies in which more structured movement programs have been inserted leads one to question their worth in *all* educational programs. Kershner[59] concluded that his hypothesis was supported when, after a program of crawling, his experimental subjects improved in crawling and in a picture identification test of I.Q., despite the fact that his control group improved more in a battery of perceptual-motor tasks (termed the Kershner revision of the Oseretsky) than did his experimental subjects! Other studies purporting to support the Doman-Delacato program of movement education are similarly questionable in content and methodology. One reviewer has suggested that the studies are distinguished only by "their faults."[38]

Robbins, in investigating the influence of the Doman-Delacato program upon the subjects' ability to distinguish left from right, to read, and to form other perceptual judgments, found that the program exerted no significant influence upon the attributes tested.[81] Laterality was not improved significantly in a program which stressed left-right and unilateral motor activity, according to Robbin's findings. His investigation is one of the few in which proper controls were utilized to study this program of motor training.

The reluctance of Doman and Delacato to subject their methods to experimental verification has made some members of the medical profession skeptical of their worth.[82,102] The extraordinary physical demands made upon the child and his family are similarly questioned by leading pediatricians, neurologists, and psychiatrists.

It is possible that some children may benefit from the Doman-Delacato method of increasing their mobility. However, to subject all children with learning problems to such a strenuous program of extensive and prolonged physical therapy is open to question.[102] An effort should be made to learn just what kind of child is being dealt with, and in what ways can the child improve under the conditions of the program, if indeed any improvement may be elicited on the part of any child under the conditions described in the literature outlining the methodology.[23,24]

The influence of the program espoused by Kephart[58] has also been scrutinized with varying degrees of sophistication. In a recent definitive study by Brown,[9] it was found that while certain measures of perception were improved, after engaging in the tasks Kephart outlines, no significant improvement in reading scores was forthcoming.* Other researchers studying the effects of training procedures espoused by Dr. Kephart have published findings which are not much more promising. Rutherford studied the effect of Kephart activities on the Metropolitan Readiness Test scores of kindergarten children, and found a significant gain for the boys but not for the girls. LaPray and Ross, using first graders who were low in both reading and visual perception, found that one group after being trained in simple reading materials improved in reading, while another group given training in large-muscle activities and visual training improved in these attributes but not in reading.[61] We have not found any well-controlled research which supports the supposition that Kephart-type activities enable groups of children to function better academically. It is probable, however, that individual children with movement problems will benefit in specific and general ways from the type of perceptual-motor training outlined by Kephart in his several publications.[57, 58] However, more research concerning these methodologies is certainly called for; particularly studies in which the influence of various components of Kephart's perceptual-motor training program are studied as isolated variables.

Kephart has made a significant contribution to the understanding and remediation of some of the perceptual-motor difficulties of neurologically impaired children. The techniques suggested in his film series and in his texts[57] offer helpful suggestions when working with children with perceptual-motor problems. However his major hypothesis, that movement is the basis of the intellect, is questionable.

Many child development experts would similarly question Kephart's concept of veridical development (the exact sequential acquisition of behavior). In truth, children develop simultaneously in several facets of behavior at the same time. They may sprint ahead in one area while remaining relatively fixed or even regressing in another area of development. Illingworth has termed this phenomenon diffusion and differentiation and the authors believe represents a truer picture of the complexities of the manner in which the child develops, than the one painted by Kephart.

Kephart,[58] Piaget,[77] and others contend that infantile reflexes somehow ''flow into voluntary movement patterns. Actually, most infantile reflexes terminate before the appearance of most voluntary movement patterns. Ausubel and others[4, 74] have correctly pointed out that reflexes and voluntary movements are divisible early in life.

Kephart also places emphasis upon the improvement of balance. He contends that poor balance reflects a defect in the cerebellum which in turn will ''short

*Scholars should probably place more faith in findings produced by experimenters without an obvious emotional commitment to the various programs and by those not in close physical proximity to the various facilities in which these programs take place, as exemplified by the investigations by Robbins [8] and Brown.[9] If advocates of the various programs engage in research purporting to establish their worth, it is like the brother of a drug manufacturer researching a drug without the traditional double-blind precautions traditional in such research.

circuit'' thought from the cortex. Research findings supporting the proposition that balance is as important as Kephart suggests are difficult to locate. Indeed, Sleeper[87] found that there was no significant relationship between balance and perceptual processes; while other research indicates that various balance measures are not predictive of each other.[31] Balance, if improved, is likely to exert a positive influence over several *motor* attributes including agility. It is unlikely, however, upon surveying the available research, that improving a child's balance will result in any marked changes in academic achievement.

MOVEMENT IN INFANCY AND EMERGING INTELLECTUAL BEHAVIOR

Another type of evidence has been advanced to support the supposition that movement undergirds the intellect. The observation that infants seem to move and to explore their environment with intensity prior to the emergence of verbal and cognitive behaviors has suggested to some that movement is the base of the pyramid with the higher associative processes at its apex.[23]

A survey of the literature in child development, particularly recent investigations of the visual and perceptual behavior of infants during the first weeks of life,[101] suggests that normal infants do seem to learn about some components of their spaceworld through movement. However, the pairing of visual-motor impressions represents only *one* combination of sensory information available to the maturing infant. There are other channels through which the infant may collect information about his world, several of which are independent from the ability to move. Some viable investigators contend that the ability to make visual discriminations emerges prior to the acquisition of controlled voluntary movements.[28] Furthermore these same investigators found that early signs of perceptual activity were more predictive of later psychological development of the child than the traditional motor measures of infantile intelligence.[28] Indeed, one investigation produced findings indicating that motor behavior was delayed from one to two weeks by enriching the visual surroundings of infants. However, when the infants began to move, even though their movements had been delayed, they engaged in significantly greater amounts of exploratory behavior.[101]

It is probable, according to Kilpatrick,[60] that infants organize their perceptions of the world about them in both direct and indirect ways. The infant moves and gains ''motor copies'' of objects with his exploring hands. However, studies of children born with deficient limbs indicate that their intellectual capacities are not necessarily impaired by the lack of opportunity to explore their environment directly.[40] There seems little doubt that normal children can similarly formulate judgments of visual space without the need for direct exploration via motor activity, but may look and think about the objects, and about events to which they are exposed.

MOVEMENT AND PERCEPTION

A number of excellent laboratory experiments, involving the resolution of visual-motor distortions have produced findings which have been interpreted by some as indicating that movement is imperative to the development of *all* perceptual judgments.[47,48] However, the experimenters involved usually take no such expansive view, and do not generalize to this extent from the findings they have obtained.[48] These studies demonstrated that self-induced movement under the control of the human subjects themselves best resolves various visual-motor distortions of place location produced when grids are inspected through prisms.[47] Passive inspection of such distorting conditions, or when the subjects' limbs were moved by the experimenter as subjects watched their own movements, through the prisms, provided less accurate responses. Studies with animals, kittens, and small monkeys similarly point to the importance of self-inspection and self-induced movement in the development of simple visual-motor responses. Cats, who were not permitted to walk through their environment during the early weeks of life, did not evidence normal blinking reactions to approaching objects, nor did they reflexly stretch for surface areas as they were lowered toward tables.[47]

These findings, however, do not offer support for the generalization that movement aids all perceptual processes. Obviously, the cognitive process is important in the organization of the spatial world of children. In one study, animal-subjects were required to make very simple spatial judgments involving near space, while in an experiment involving human-subjects, no information about which they could *think* prior to performing the required tasks was given to them.

It is likely that if a group of individuals were added to such studies and were told for example that, ''the prisms make the grid seem 3 inches to the left'', as they attempted to locate intersecting lines by touching them, their performance would approximate that of the subjects who could simply move their hands or their total bodies within the distorting conditions. Indeed the experimenters placed little control over the speed and changes in velocity with which the subjects could make these various ''self-induced movements''. Thus there was little control exerted over the sensory information upon which subjects' hypothesis testing at the *cognitive level* may have been based.[47]

The findings of an investigation carried out sixty years ago support the supposition that humans can cognitively interpret the nature of visually distorting conditions (inspecting a target through water) to which they are exposed, resulting in the resolution of the distortion.[56]

Subjects in Kilpatrick's studies were able to solve the familiar distorted room illusion when they were able to move a stick or throw a ball around the room or when *they were permitted to watch another individual throw a ball or move a stick.*[60]

Thus, studies in which humans are able to resolve visual-motor distortions to which they are exposed provide information about specific kinds of motor acts as they interact with specific perceptual judgments. However, caution should be used in generalizing from these findings and in attempting to explain the manner in which normal infants form all perceptual judgments.

Factorial studies of visual perception suggest that children and adults evidence several discrete and separate attributes. The investigations by Smith[91] demonstrate the existence of four unrelated personality traits, including the ability to track movement in space, visual acuity, the ability to fractionalize space (estimate what is one-half between there and here), and the ability to make various size-distance judgments.

Similarly, factorial studies of motor attributes carried out by Fleishman and his colleagues over a period of fifteen years have demonstrated the complexity of the trait structure contained within the totality of motor behavior.[30, 31] Therefore, it is inaccurate to declare that movement, a multi-faceted complexity, positively influences perception, which is also composed of several separate human attributes. Instead, individuals purporting to aid perception through movement should delineate the exact perceptual attributes which are to be modified by specific movement tasks.

TENSION, AROUSAL AND LEARNING

Because subtle muscular tensions are sometimes recorded when people engaged in profound thought, some theorists[58] suggest that motor activity is the basis of the intellect.

A survey of the literature again provides tentative answers to the relationships existing among muscular tensions, arousal level, orienting behavior, and learning.[25, 83, 105, 65]

It is apparent that good emotional stability, intelligence, and perceptual competence are evidenced by individuals who are capable of *adjusting* their arousal level to that appropriate to the tasks confronting them. It is true that muscular tensions frequently accompany intellectual efforts. However, such tensions are merely one of a number of physiological signs that the organism is girding itself for some general effort. They do not support a causative relationship existing between thought and muscular activity.

There are innumerable investigations supporting the hypothesis that the extent to which a child or adult can control his own activity and arousal level is indicative of good intellectual performance. Studies carried out over thirty years ago have found that extra muscular tension, induced, for example, by requiring subjects to grip hand dynometers, results in an improvement in the ability to make perceptual discriminations quickly and to memorize word and letter sequences.[18, 33, 84] Conversely, contemporary studies with retardates and normal children contain findings which suggest that too high a level of activation can impede learning. In one investigation, for example, children who were unable, or unwilling, to sit still (measured by a force platform imbedded in a chair) were found to be less capable learners than were retardates who remained relatively fixed when seated.[83] Another investigation using normal children contains moderate correlations between I.Q. scores and those collected when the children were asked to move as slowly as possible in a variety of tasks ("walk from here to there as slowly as you can . . . pull the cart toward yourself slowly, draw a line slowly, etc.").[67]

Harrison similarly found that, following a program of relaxation training, children's learning capacities improved.[45]

One important goal of individuals working with children in motor activities should be to help them learn to place themselves under effective control. It is possible that relaxation training applied to some children in the gymnasium will result in increased attention span and better learning in the classroom (See Chapter 5).

Thus, again delineation of exact parameters must be made when speaking of extraneous muscular tensions and their statistical and causal relationships to thought. There is an optimum level of arousal* necessary for the performance of a given playground or classroom task. The child who is unable to adjust himself to an adequate arousal level frequently has learning difficulties. The child who can control himself, if no other problems are present, uses his intellectual potential more fully and, at the same time, will usually perform better in playground skills.

Ayres has suggested that distractibility in some children with perceptual-motor problems may be reduced by heightening their tactual awareness by stroking their skin. She suggests that hyperactive behavior and a seeming retreat from other children and learning situations may be controlled by exposing a child to non-threatening tactual stimulation of this nature. It is furthermore hypothesized that the apparent defensiveness in some hyperactive children with learning difficulties may be caused by damage to certain inhibiting centers of brain tissue which may be somewhat overcome by various brushing and stroking techniques.

Ayres cites a correlation of .54 between measures of tactile perception and tactile defensiveness on the part of children tested (based upon statements such as ''I hate this game''). She suggests, however, that additional research is needed to explore the manner in which heightened tactile sensitivity and tolerance for tactual stimulation interacts with learning and hyperactivity before definitive statements can be made concerning the worth of this technique.[5]

Zeaman and House have theorized, as the result of a number of experimental studies, that learning problems are likely to be caused by lack of attention to appropriate stimuli than to the inability to discriminate and to otherwise deal with the complexity of the task's components.[105] While other experimenters have taken issue with this simplistic explanation for learning difficulties,[103] it does seem true that many children cannot learn, because they cannot attend to learning tasks.

VISUAL TRAINING

Although the focus of the text is upon motor activity, an ancillary portion of many motor education programs involves visual training. It is difficult to teach motor activities without a parallel exercise of ocular capacities for as a child watches his own limbs, or tracks the ball thrown to him, his eyes are involved in the activity. Programs of visual training are encouraged primarily by the Optometric Extension Program within the United States. Getman[36,37] has published a methodology based upon the theoretical speculation that visual training will remediate educational difficulties.

It is surprising that, within the many years during which these practices have been engaged in, so few definitive studies have been produced attending to their

---

*Arousal and activation are similar concepts indicative of the appearance of a group of physiological and psychological indices that the organism is preparing itself for some kind of threat and/or intellectual and/or physical activity. Emotional arousal may or may not be accompanied by excesses of muscular tension....however, arousal for perceived action and difficult intellectual efforts are usually accompanied by tension changes in the large trunk muscles.

worth. Inspection of the literature suggests a conflict between findings in which individual subjects have evidenced marked improvement in ocular and accompanying perceptual and academic performance, and data from studies in which group changes fail to emerge after visual-training has been applied en masse.

There seems little doubt that certain parameters of ocular efficiency are important to learning. Tests of the tracking ability of the eyes of children entering school and tests of fine and gross motor coordination may predict in a general way those who may later be expected to experience spelling and reading problems.[13,88] However, a test of ocular efficiency in itself may not be a reliable way of predicting reading failure.

Various indices of ocular inefficiencies are found to be more common among children with reading problems than in populations of children who read well.[63,66] However, there is little available evidence to delineate exactly how much ocular malfunction is necessary before reading will be impaired.[63] Some children read well, yet their ability to accommodate, to track, and to otherwise use their visual apparatus is deficient, while other children with no visual problems have learning difficulties.

Several conflicting views regarding ocular difficulties are found in professional literature. Some observers suggest the inaccurate visual movements of the reader, as he scans a page, handicaps his reading and comprehension. Others speculate that a child with cognitive disturbances is searching in vain through the written material for understanding;[63] for this reason, his eyes tend to jump irrationally from word to word. Smith[89] and others have suggested that the inability of severely disabled readers to fixate in ordinary home and school tasks may be stress related, and is a primary source of variability during tasks involving visual discrimination. These conflicting reports concerning the relationship of ocular malfunction to various academic parameters suggest that with our present state of knowledge, each child with learning disabilities be subjected to a thorough examination in which the many facets of ocular function and visual perception are evaluated.

Efficient visual tracking may not be such a critical quality underlying reading as it is currently thought to be. Studies dating from the 1870's indicate that the eyes of a reader move in starts and jerks from word to word, and they are fixed from 70 to 90 per cent of the time.[97] Good ocular control may be necessary to regulate stopping at the places on the pages at which the reader desires to look.[63] The research indicates that failure in near-point fusion is more prevalent among children with reading difficulties. At the same time as children mature, and/or become more proficient readers, the number of fixations per 100 words decreases sharply. Similar to the other processes discussed in these pages, reading comprehension and visual perception are more complicated than some proponents of visual-motor training would have us believe. Reading is not dependent solely upon the ability to smoothly move the eyes from side to side. Reading proficiency involves the interaction of several complex processes involving: form recognition, the ability to organize space, the ability to interpret a series of stimuli, near-point fusion, and finally the ability to translate word-shapes into concepts.

The causes for poor reading are probably as numerous as the causes of retardation itself (estimated at from 70 to 80). Severe ocular malfunction undoubtedly will impair some children when reading. However, there are other portions of the processes described which, if deficient, will impede the child's ability to translate the written page into terms meaningful to him.

HAND AND EYE PREFERENCE

Attention within visual-motor programs is often directed toward the purported problem of cross-dominance (hand preference differs from the eye preference in one-eyed tasks). Such programs assume that malfunctioning peripheral ocular processes are of more importance than the central processes in reading with comprehension, whereas in truth, a strong case can be made for the proposition that reading involves the translation of a visual configuration into a verbal-cognitive symbol. Studies by Belmont and Birch[8] and by L. Smith[90] indicate that the incidence of cross-dominance is as prevalent in populations of normal children as in groups of children with learning difficulties. An investigation by Stephens, Cunningham, and Stigler recently found no relationship between cross-dominance and reading readiness in kindergarten children.[95]

A student under our direction just completed a study in which he found that cross-dominance was as prevalent within a population of poor readers who evidenced signs of concomitant neurological impairment as was present in a group of poor readers who did not have neurological "soft-signs." The findings of this study, similar to those produced by other investigators, suggested that cross-dominance is not one of a series of neurological deficits sometimes seen in children with reading problems. Forty per cent of the people in the United States are left-eyed, while 10 to 15 per cent of the people are left-handed, and these are not necessarily the same people.[41] Thus, cross-dominance within recent years is eliciting less concern among well-informed educators.

The failure to establish hand preference has been cited by some as a critical block to the intellectual process. However, a survey of the literature reveals that animals at all points on the evolutionary scale evidence asymmetrical paw, claw, and leg usage.[41] A grasshopper's preferred leg must be removed before it will begin to scratch with the other one. Further, rats, evidencing paw preference, could not be trained out of that preference according to a 1930 study. Therefore, it is not surprising to find a human evidencing a variety of asymmetric functions as he walks, uses his upper limbs and his eyes.[75, 76, 98, 15]

While it is true that children with learning problems often have difficulty establishing a hand preference, it is similarly true that they adopt inefficient work methods when attempting to engage in most of life's activities. Despite the lack of evidence to support the importance of establishing hand preference, it is true that a child confronted with a unilateral task such as writing needs to select one hand. For this reason, it is appropriate for educators to assess hand preference. Techniques for accomplishing this are outlined on page 6.

SUMMARY

A review of the literature dealing with relationships to be found among perception, motion, and academic achievement as well as the other components of academic efforts and of related attributes leads to the following conclusions.

1. **Movement** activities will aid a child to think to that extent to which he

thinks about the sequence, variety, and nature of the movements in which he is engaged.

2. Motor tasks may aid in the development of certain perceptual attributes. Visual-motor coordination is important to accurate hand movement for writing and drawing.

3. Improved motor task proficiency, reflected in better fitness and sport skills, may result in the increased academic performance of some children with learning problems, because their self-concept has been enhanced.

4. Movement experiences, if properly applied, may help some hyperactive children to place themselves under better control which will, in turn, lead toward increased competency in classroom tasks.

5. Visual training may aid some children to learn better if a careful visual examination precedes such training and if the components of the training program are applied to the remediation of the specific deficits identified in such an evaluation.

6. Structured movement programs in which creeping and crawling are employed are of questionable value in the remediation of anything but severe motor ineptitude.

7. Helpful to the identification of children with potential reading problems are measures of (a) drawing; (b) scores obtained from measures of coordination tasks collected from pre-school children; (c) evaluation of various visual attributes.

Primary conflicts between observed changes in individual children and the findings of research studies in which group change is usually surveyed are reconcilable. In the future it is believed that communication between clinicians and experimentalists will be improved if the latter taken into consideration individual differences within their subject-populations, rather than studying groups of undefined children to whom general labels are assigned.

REFERENCES

1. Abercrombie, J. J., Gardiner, P. A., Hanson, E., Jockheere, J., Lindon, R. L., Solomon, G., and Tyson, M. C.: "Visual, Perceptual and Visuomotor Impairment in Physically Handicapped Children," *Percept. & Mot. Skills,* (Monograph Supplement±, *3,* 18, 1964.

2. American Academy of Pediatrics Executive Board Statement: "Doman-Delacato Treatment of Neurologically Handicapped Children," AAP News Letters, 11–16, Dec., 1965.

3. Anderson, J. E.: "The Limitations of Infant and Pre-School Tests in the Measurement of Intelligence," *J. Psychol: 8,* 351–379, 1939.

4. Ausubel, David P.: "A Critique of Piaget's Theory of the Ontogenesis of Motor Behavior," *J. Genet. Psychol.: 109,* 119–122, 1966.

5. Ayres, Jean A.: "Interrelation of Perception, Function, and Treatment," *American Physical Therapy Association,* 46–47, July, 1966.

6. Balow, I., and Balow, B.: "Lateral Dominance and Reading Achievement in the Second Grade," *Am. Ed. Res. J.; I,* 139–143, 1964.

7. Bayley N.: "Consistency and Variability in the Growth of Intelligence From Birth to Eighteen Years," *J. Genet. Psychol.: 75,* 96, 1965.

8. Belmont, L. and Birch, H.: "Lateral Dominance, Lateral Awareness and Reading Disability," *Child Dev.: 36,* 57–71, 1965.
9. Brown, Roscoe C.: "The Effect of a Perceptual-Motor Education Program on Perceptual-Motor Skills and Reading Readiness," Speech presented at research section, AAHPER Convention, St. Louis, Missouri, April 1, 1968.
10. Carlson, Paul V. and Greenspoon, Morton K.: "The Uses and Abuses of Visual Training for Children With Perceptual Motor Learning Problems," Summary of a paper presented to the California Optometric Association Meeting, San Francisco, Feb., 1967.
11. Cattel, P.: "Constant Changes in the Stanford-Binet, I.Q.; *J. Ed. Psychol.: 22,* 544–550, 1931.
12. Cavanaugh, M. C. *et al.:* "Prediction from the Cattel Infant Intelligence Scale," *J. Consult. Psychol.: 21,* 33–37, 1957.
13. Chang, T. M. C. and Chang, V. A. C.: "Relation of Visual-Motor Skill and Reading Achievement in Primary Grade Pupils of Superior Ability," *Percept. & Mot. Skills: 24,* 51–53, 1967.
14. Clausen, Johannes: *Ability Structure and Subgroups in Mental Retardation,* Washington, D.C., Spartan Books, 1966.
15. Cole, J.: "Paw Preference in Cats Related to Hand Preference in Animals and Man," *J. Comp. & Physio. Psychol.: 48,* 137–145, 1955.
16. Cohen, Abraham: "Hand Preference and Developmental Status of Infants," *J. Genet. Psychol.: 108,* 337–345, 1966.
17. Corder, W. D.: "Effects of Physical Education on the Intellectual, Physical, and Social Development of Educable Mentally Retarded Boys," Unpublished special project, Nashville, Tennessee, George Peabody College, 1965.
18. Courts, F. A.: "Relation Between Experimentally Induced Muscular Tension and Memorization," *J. Exp. Psychol.: 25,* 107, 235–256, 1939.
19. Cratty, Bryant J.: *Movement Behavior and Motor Learning,* 2nd Ed., Philadelphia, Lea & Febiger, 1967.
20. ———: *Developmental Sequences of Perceptual-Motor Tasks and Movement Activities for Neurological Handicapped and Retarded Children and Youth,* Freeport, L.I., New York, Educational Activities, Inc., 1967.
21. ———: *The Perceptual-Motor Attributes of Mentally Retarded Children and Youth,* Los Angeles County Mental Retardation Services Board, August, 1966.
22. Davis, R. A.: *Psychology of Learning,* New York, McGraw-Hill Book Co., 1935.
23. Delacato, Carl H.: *The Treatment and Prevention of Reading Problems,* Springfield, Charles C Thomas, 1959.
24. ———: *The Diagnosis and Treatment of Speech and Reading Problems,* Springfield, Charles C Thomas, 1963.
25. Duffy, E.: "The Psychological Significance of the Concept of Arousal of 'Activiation'," *Psychol. Rev.: 64,* 265–275, 1957.
26. Fait, H. F. and Kupferes, H. J.: "A Study of Two Motor Achievement Tests and Their Implications in Planning Physical Education Activities for the Mentally Retarded," *Am. J. Ment. Defic.: 60–64,* 729–732, April, 1956.
27. Fantz, Robert L.: "The Origin of Form Perception," *Sci. Am.: 204,* 459–475, 1961.
28. ———: "Pattern Discrimination and Selective Attention as Determinants of Perceptual Development from Birth," in *Perceptual Development in Children,* Aline H. Kidd and Jeanne L. Rivoire, (Eds.), New York, International Universities Press, Inc., 1966.
29. Finch, G.: "Chimpanzee Handedness," *Science, 194,* 117–118, 1941.
30. Fleishman, Edwin A. and Ellison, Gaylor D.: "A Factor Analysis of Fine Manipulative Tests," *J. Applied Psychol.: 46,* 95–105, 1962.
31. Fleishman, Edwin A., Thomas, Paul, and Munroe, Philip: "The Dimensions of Physical

Fitness: A Factor Analysis of Speed Flexibility, Balance and Coordination Tests," Technical Report No. 3 The Office of Naval Research, Department of Psychology, Yale University, September, 1961.

32. Francis, R. J., and Rarick, G. L.: "Motor Characteristics of the Mentally Retarded," U.S. Office of Education Cooperative Research Project No. 152 (6432), University of Wisconsin, September 16, 1967.

33. Freeman, G. L.: "Changes in Tonus During Complete and Interrupted Mental Work," *J. Genet. Psychol.: 4,* 309–334, 1930.

34. Gagne, Robert M. (Ed.): *Learning and Individual Differences,* Columbus, Ohio, Charles E. Merrill Books, Inc., 1967.

35. Getman, G. N.: "How to Develop Your Child's Intelligence," Luverne, Minnesota, G. N. Getman, 1962.

36. Getman, G. N. and Kane, Elmer R.: *The Physiology of Readiness,* Minneapolis, Minnesota, Programs to Accelerate School Success, 1963.

37. ———: "The Physiology of Readiness Experiment," Minneapolis, P.A.S.S. Inc., Programs to Accelerate School Success, 1963.

38. Glass, Gene V. and Robbins, Melvin P.: "A Critique on the Role of Neurological Organization in Reading Performance," *Read. Res. Quart.: 3,* 5–52, 1967.

39. Gorelick, Molly C.: "The Effectiveness of Visual Form Training in a Prereading Program, *J. Ed. Res.: 57–58,* 315–318, March, 1965.

40. Guarin-Decarie T.: "The Mental and Educational Development of Thalidomide Children," Inter-Clinic Information Service, Committee of Prosthetic Research and Development, Jan. 1968.

41. Hecaen, Henry and Ajuriaguerra, Julian De: *Left-Handedness Manual Superiority and Cerebral Dominance,* translated by Eric Ponder, New York, Grune & Stratton, 1964.

42. Haring, Norris G. and Stables, Jeanne Marie: "The Effect of Gross Motor Development on Visual Perception and Hand-Eye Coordination," *Am. Phys. Therapy Assn.: 42–46,* 129–135, Feb., 1966.

43. Harris, A. J.: "What About Special Theories of Teaching Remedial Reading?" Current Issues Program, Boston, Mass., International Reading Association Convention, April, 1968.

44. Harris, Charles S.: "Perceptual Adaptation to Inverted Reversal and Displaced Vision," *Psychol. Rev.: 72–76,* 419–444, 1954.

45. Harrison, W., Lecrone, H. Temerlin, M. K., and Trousdale, W.: "The Effect of Music and Exercise Upon the Self-Help Skills of Non-Verbal Retardates, *Am. J. Ment. Defic.: 71–72,* 279–282, 1966.

46. Harrington, S. M. J., and Durrell, D. D.: "Mental Maturity Versus Perception Abilities in Primary Reading," *J. Ed. Psychol.: 46,* 375–380, 1955.

47. Held, Richard: "Plasticity in Sensory-Motor Systems," *Sci. Am.: 1–9,* 213–215, 1965.

48. Held, Richard and Mikaelian, H.: "Motor-Sensory Feedback Versus Need in Adaptation to Rearrangement," *Percept. & Mot. Skills: 18,* 685–688, 1964.

49. Howard, I. B. and Templeton, W. B.: *Human Spatial Orientation,* New York, John Wiley & Sons, 1966.

50. Illingworth, R. S.: *The Development of the Infant and Young Child,* Normal and Abnormal, 3rd Ed. Edinburgh, E. & S. Livingston, Ltd., 1967.

51. Ismail, A. H. and Gruber, J. J.: *Motor Aptitude and Intellectual Performance,* Columbus, Ohio, Charles E. Merrill, 1968.

52. Javel, E.: "Essai sur la physiologie de la lecture," *Annu. -'Oculist: 81,* 61–73, 1879.

53. Johnson, G. O. R.: "A Study of the Social Position of Mentally Handicapped Children in the Regular Grades," *Am. J. Ment. Defic.: 55,* 60–89, 1950.

54. Johnson, P. W.: "The Relation of Certain Anomalies of Vision and Lateral Dominance to Reading Disability," *Mono. Soc. Res. Child Dev.: 7-2,* 1942.

55. Jones, M. H., Dayton, G. O., Didon, L. V. and Leton, D. A.: Reading Readiness Studies: Suspect First Graders," *Percept. & Mot. Skills: 23,* 103-112, 1966.

56. Judd, C. H.: "The Relationship of Special Training to General Intelligence," *Ed. Rev.: 26,* 28-42, 1908.

57. Kephart, Newell C.: "Perceptual-Motor Aspects of Learning Disabilities," *Except. Child.: 31-34,* 201-206, 1964.

58. ———: *The Slower Learner in the Classroom,* Columbus, Ohio, Charles E. Merrill Books, Inc., 1956.

59. Kershner, John R.: "Doman-Delacato's Theory of Neurological Organization Applied with Retarded Children," *Except. Child:* 441-450, Feb., 1968.

60. Kilpatrick, F. P.: "Two Processes in Perceptual Learning," *J. Exp. Psychol.: 47,* 362-370, 1954.

61. LaPray, M. and Ross, R.: "Auditory and Visual-Perceptual Training," in *Vistas in Reading,* Ed. J. Allen Figural, International Reading Association Conference Proceedings, *XI,* 530-532, 1966.

62. Leighton, J., Cupp, M., Prince, A., Philadaum, D., and McLarren, M.: "The Effect of a Physical Fitness Development Program on Self-concept, Mental Age, and Job Proficiency in the Mentally Retarded," *J. Of Physio. & Ment. Rehab: 20,* 4-11, 1966.

63. Leton, Donald A.: "Visual-Motor Capacities and Ocular Efficiency in Reading," *Percept. & Mot. Skills: 15,* 407-432, 1962.

64. Luria, A. R. and Vinogradova, Olga S.: "An Objective Investigation of the Dynamics of Semantic Systems," *Br. J. Psychol.: 50,* 89-105, 1959.

65. Lynn, R.: *Attention, Arousal and the Orientation Reaction,* New York, Pergamon Press, 1966.

66. Lyons, C. V. and Lyons, Emily B.: "The Power of Visual Training, As Measured in Factors of Intelligence," *J. Am. Optometric Assn.:* 255-262, Dec., 1954.

67. Maccoby, Eleanor E., Dowley, Edith M., and Hagen, John W.: "Activity Level and Intellectual Functioning in Normal Pre-School Children," *Child Dev.: 36,* 761-769, 1965.

68. Maltzman, I., and Rasking, D. C.: "Effects of Individual Differences in the Orienting Reflex on Conditioning and Complex Processes," *J. Exp. Res. Personal.: I,* 1-16, 1965.

69. Mosston, Muska: *Teaching Physical Education,* Columbus, Ohio, Charles E. Merrill Books, Inc., 1966.

70. Neale, Marie, D.: "The Effects of a Broad 'Art' and Movement Program Upon a Group of 'Trainable' Retarded Children," International Copenhagen Congress on the Scientific Study of Mental Retardation, Denmark, 7-14, 1964.

71. Oliver, J. N.: "The Effect of Physical Conditioning Exercises and Activities on the Mental Characteristics of Educationally Sub-Normal Boys," *Br. J. Ed. Psychol.: 28,* 155-165, June, 1958.

72. Orton, Samuel Torrey: *Reading, Writing and Speech Problems in Children,* New York, W. W. Norton Co., Inc., 1937.

73. Park, G. E.: "Reading Difficulty (Dyslexia) from the Opthalmic Point of View," *Am. J. Ophthalmol.: 31,* 28-34, 1948.

74. Peiper, A.: *Cerebral Function in Infancy and Childhood,* Consultants Bureau, New York, 1963.

75. Peterson, G. M.: "Mechanisms of Handedness in the Rat," *Comp. Monograph: 9,* 1-67, 1934.

76. ———: "Transfer in Handedness in the Rat from Forced Practice," *J. Comp. Physiol. Psychol.: 44,* 184-190, 1951.

77. Piaget, Jean and Inhelder, Barbel: *The Child's Conception of Space,* London, Toutledge and Keagan Paul, 1963.
78. Radler, D. H.: "Visual Training Hopeful-Now Johnny Can Read," *Horizon: 3,* 13–18, 1956.
79. Roach, E. G. and Kephart, N. C.: *The Purdue Perceptual-Motor Survey,* Charles E. Merrill Books, Inc., Columbus, Ohio, 1966.
80. Robbins, Melvyn, P.: "A Study of the Validity of Delacato's Theory of Neurological Organization," *Except. Child: 32,* 617–623, April 17, 1966.
81. ———: "The Delacato Interpretation of Neurological Organization," *Except. Child: 32,* 523–617, April 17- 1966.
82. ———: "Letter to the Editor," *Except. Child: 33,* 200–201, November, 1966.
83. Semmel, M. I.: "Arousal Theory and Vigilance Behavior of Educable Mentally Retarded and Average Children," *Am. J. Ment. Defic.: 70,* 38–47, 1965.
84. Shaw, W. A.: "Facilitating Effects of Induced Tension Upon the Perception Span for Digits," *J. Exp. Psychol.: 51,* 113–117, 1956.
85. Singer, G. and Day, R. H.: "The Effects of Special Judgments on the Perceptual After-effects Resulting from Prismatically Transformed Vision," *Aust. J. Psychol.: 18*-1, 1966.
86. Singer, Robert N. and Brink, J. W.: "Relation of Perceptual-Motor Ability and Intellectual Ability in Elementary School Children," *Percept. & Mot. Skills: 24,* 967–970, 1967.
87. Sleeper, Mildred: "Body Balance and Space Perception," M. S. Thesis, Unpublished, University of Southern California, 1965.
88. Smith, C. and Keogh, B.: "The Group Bender Gestalt as a Reading Readiness Screening Instrument:, *Percept. & Mot. Skills: 15,* 639–645, 1962.
89. Smith, D. E. P. and Semmelroth, C.: "Micro-Movements During Apparent Fixations in Reading, *Yearbook of Nat'l Reading Conference,* U. of Michigan, *3, 4,* 188–194, 1964–65.
90. Smith, L.: "A Study of Laterality Characteristics of Retarded Readers and Reading Achievers," *J. Exp. Ed.: 18,* 321–329, 1950.
91. Smith, O. W. and Smith, Patricia-C.: "Developmental Studies of Spatial Judgments by Children and Adults," *Percept. & Mot. Skills: 22,* 3–73, 1966.
92. Sokolov, E. N.: "Neuronal Models and the Orienting Reflex," In *The Central Nervous System and Behavior,* Mary A. B. Brazier (Ed.), New York, Josiah Macy, Jr. Foundation, 187–276, 1960.
93. Solomon, A., and Prangle, R.: "Demonstrations of Physical Fitness Improvement in the EMR, *Except. Child: 33,* 177–181, November, 1967.
94. Start, K. B.: "The Influence of Subjectively Assessed Games Ability on Gain in Motor Performance After Mental Practice," *J. Genet. Psychol.: 67,* 169–173, 1962.
95. Stephens, W. E.; Cunningham, E., and Stigler, B. J.: "Reading Readiness and Eye-Hand Preference Patterns in First Grade Children," *Except. Child: 30,* 481–488, March, 1968.
96. Thompson, M. E.: "A Study of Reliabilities of Selected Gross Muscular Coordination Test Items," *Human Resources Res. Cen. Res. Bull.: 52*–59, 1952.
97. Tinker, M. A.: "The Study of Eye Movements in Reading," *Psychol. Bull.: 43,* 93–120, 1946.
98. Tsai, L. and Maurer, S.: "Right Handedness in White Rats," *Science: 74,* 436–438, 1930.
99. Weatherford, R. S. and Horrocks, J.: "Peer Acceptance and Over and Under Achievement in School, *J. Psychol.: 66,* 215–220, 1967.
100. Whilden, Peggy P.: "Comparison of Two Methods of Teaching Beginning Basketball," *Res. Quart.: 27,* 235–242, 1956.

101. White, Burton L. and Held, Richard: "Plasticity of Sensori-motor Development in the Human Infant," *The* Causes of Behavior: Readings in Child Development and Educational Psychology: Judy F. Rosenblith, and Wesley Allin-Smith (Eds.), Boston, Allyn & Bacon Inc., 1966.

102. Whitsell, Leon J.: "Delacato's 'Neurological Organization': A Medical Appraisal," *California School Health, 3,* 1–13, Fall, 1967.

103. Wickens, Delos D.: "The Orienting Reflex and Attention" in *Learning and Individual Differences,* Gagne, R. M. (Ed.), Merrill International Psychology Series, Columbus, Ohio, 1967.

104. Wischner, George J.: "Individual Differences in Retardate Learning," Learning and Individual Differences, Robert M. Gagne, (Ed.), Columbus, Ohio, Charles E. Merrill Books, Inc., 1967, 193–213.

105. Zeaman, D. and Orlando, R.: "The Role of Attention in Retardate Discrimination Learning," *Handbook of Mental Deficiency,* N. R. Ellis (Ed.), New York, McGraw-Hill Book Co., 159–223, 1963.

3

Movement Attributes and Performance Capacities in Infants and Children

To evaluate a child who is suspected of possessing various perceptual-motor problems, an understanding should be obtained of the perceptual-motor attributes connected with movement which *normally* may be expected as a child matures. One purpose of this chapter is to present a review of when certain observable behaviors appear during the initial years of a child's life. The final portion of the chapter contains norms of more exact performance measures to which an individual child's performance may be compared.

Several considerations should be kept in mind when reviewing the following material. An individual child may evidence motor attributes which are at variance with the accepted norms, and still be considered a "normal" child. His inability to perform as expected may simply indicate that he needs more experience in a given type of activity, or special help which will enable him to overcome the gap between his performance and the suggested norms. Not only may a child evidence behavior different from that expected, but also he may regress in his ability to perform efficiently a given task or a group of tasks as he matures. When evaluating a child, several variables may influence scores: (*a*). The presence of an observer may upset the child; (*b*) the child may be distracted by the objects he must use; (*c*) the child's momentary level of excitation and/or the presence of a model to be imitated may create problems for him. Thus, indices of a child's perceptual-motor maturation do not always appear in the neat sequences sometimes outlined in the child development literature.

However, if a child evidences marked delay in the acquisition of important movement attributes, professional personnel should give the child a complete physical and psychological assessment as well as an evaluation of his perceptual-motor processes. As soon as his movement problems are identified, a remediation program should be carried out.

MOVEMENT ATTRIBUTES

Body-Image. Some specialists do not consider accurate verbal identifications of body-parts as "movement attributes" and indeed they are not. However, several kinds of close relationships exist between the body-image (evaluated by direct responses to verbal directions to move in various ways, or to touch various body parts) and movement itself. Frequently, a close correlation exists between measures of body-image and scores obtained on motor ability tests.[5] Consistent findings indicate that movement activities enhance measurable aspects of the body-image.[9] Very often children with movement problems evidence a concomitant inability accurately to identify body parts, left-right dimensions of the body, and to make similar judgments. Thus, programs in perceptual-motor education frequently contain activities which purport to enhance the body-image. The sequences in Chart 1 are the results of research by Ilg and Ames,[9] Belmont and Birch,[2] and in studies carried out by Cratty[5] and his students.

To many, the concept of body-image is a global one, encompassing the totality of percepts, concepts, and feelings formed about the body. Attempts to evaluate the body-image have been carried out by asking children (*a*) to verbally identify body parts;[3] (*b*) to imitate the gestures of an experiment;[4] (*c*) to construct a mannequin;[1] and (*d*) to draw a person.[10]

Although a single measure of the body-image has yet to be developed which will satisfy all theorists interested in this elusive concept, the following norms are based upon responses to verbal requests to move in various ways, and to point to various body parts. Admittedly, these data may be primarily a measure of vocabulary rather than an accurate assessment of percepts concerning the body itself. Chart 1 contains three "channels" involving: (*a*) verbal identification of larger body-parts; (*b*) verbal identification of hands; (*c*) identification of various left-right dimensions of the body with related left-right judgments.

Dealing with Objects. Within the first few hours of birth, an infant may be distracted by an object. Within the first weeks, he will begin to watch his hand, and by the third month, he may begin to swipe and to corral objects. Later, this inaccurate behavior will become more refined as he manipulates objects with his hands and mouth. Manipulative behavior is an important channel through which children gain information about their world. The following sequence recorded in Chart 2 was obtained by inspection of the work of Uzgiris,[16] Halverson[8] Piaget,[13] Gesell,[7] White and Held,[17] and others.

A sequence of this nature not only permits a reasonably exact evaluation of one aspect of a child's perceptual-motor development, but at the same time suggests a helpful educational sequence for children with severe movement problems (*i.e.,* cerebral palsy). The sequence is initiated by behaviors which involve orienting reactions to the presence of objects, and to the child's hand itself. The progressive sequence begins with the first weeks of a child's life and terminates when his behavior suggests the emergence of conceptualization on the part of the maturing child, including the integration of his verbal and social behavior with his manipulative acts.

Throwing and Catching. Two theories are advanced for the emergence of throwing behavior in children. Some suggest that throwing evolves from an in-

Chart 1

AGE (In years)	VERBAL IDENTIFICATION OF BODY PARTS	THE HANDS	THE LEFT AND RIGHT
0		watches hands move	
1	stomach, head, parts of face, limbs.	identifies hands, fingers, toes	
2			
3	objects in relationship to body planes, *i.e.,* "things are in front, back, to the side of me."	identifies thumb, little finger, first finger.	knows words "right" and "left", but not that they are on opposite sides of body.
4			
5	shoulders, elbows, knees	identifies middle and ring finger	knows right and left are on opposite sides, but is unable to tell which is which
6	trunk appears in drawings; thighs, forearms, etc. identified		some left-right judgments made accurately
7	wrists, ankles, shins, parts of limbs identified		more left-right judgments on self and in letters, numbers, etc. made correctly
8			can identify the left and right of other people when facing them.
9			can describe the left-right movement of others while watching them
10			

Chart 2

AGE (In Months)	SELECTED BEHAVIORS
1–3	Looks at objects.
2–4	Beginning control of one and/or both arms.
2–4	Arm-waving and other indices of excitation when in the presence of persons and/or objects.
2–4	Examines hand for prolonged periods of time.
2–4	Alternately examines hand and then the object present.
2–4	Corrals objects placed on surfaces in front of him; swipes at objects placed overhead.
2–4	Inspects both hands simultaneously in front of face.
3–5	Slowly brings hand to objects and touches them, alternately glancing at object and hand in the process.
3–5	Hand preference emerges.
5–8	Grasps objects with crude grip, using palms and all fingers placed together.
5–12	Brings objects to mouth for examination by lips, tongue, and inner mouth surfaces.
6–9	Grasps objects with fingers, examines things tactually.
6–+	Exploits objects: hits, stacks, shakes them, begins to let go of objects using crude forms of throwing.
7–+	Begins to search for objects which drop out of view.
10–+	Shows objects to others to instigate social behavior and to get a response.
16–+	Names objects and begins to classify them.

Chart 3

Throwing and Catching Form

AGE (In years-months)	THROWING	CATCHING
2-3	Stiff-arm movement of arm from front to back without body movement.	Stops rolling ball, able to catch large ball but with stiff elbows.
3.6-5	Shift of body weight toward throw.	Elbows in front of body with hands in vice-like position.
5.6-6	Step forward with foot on same side as throwing arm.	
6.6+	Step forward with foot opposite to that of throwing arm.	Mature catching pattern with elbows at the side of the body.

herent pattern which was a necessity to the preservation of life on the part of our evolutionary ancestors. A second explanation suggests that throwing occurs accidentally at first; when holding an object, if a child moves his hand rapidly, cen-

Chart 4

Throwing and Catching, Selected Performance Measures

AGE (In years)	CATCHING*	THROWING DISTANCE
2	2 out of 5 trials	4-5 feet
3	3 out of 5 trials	6-7 feet
4	4 out of 5 trials	8-9 feet
5	5 out of 5 trials	10-11 feet
6		14-17 feet

*The Measure: Ball circumference 16 inches
Ball is bounced chest high to child from distance of 15 feet away
Total number of trials is 5

trifical force will dislodge it. The sound made as the object strikes something, provides the reinforcement needed for additional attempts.

The developmental sequences outlined in Chart 3 were obtained from research by Wild [18] and others, as well as from summaries by Espenschade and Eckert. [6]

SEQUENTIAL DEVELOPMENT OF LOCOMOTOR ACTIVITIES

In addition to those motor attributes involving the use of the upper limbs, children evidence degrees of proficiency in the use of their lower limbs. Charts 5, 6, 7 and 8 illustrate the sequential development of: beginning locomotor behavior, hopping, rhythmic hopping, jumping, galloping, and skipping.

Behavior Leading to Walking.   The infant is born with a number of birth reflexes, one of which resembles walking. Soon after birth, however, many of these reflex patterns terminate, and only much later does the child evidence the ability to engage in voluntary locomotion. The progression in Chart 5 summarizes material taken from Shirley, [14] Gesell, [7] McGraw, [12] and several other authorities. [6, 13]

Jumping.   The jumping pattern begins with a one-foot take off, followed by a short period when the body is not supported, ending with a landing on the other foot. Jumping from one foot and landing on two feet occurs next, followed by controlled jumps from both feet, with varying degrees of arm involvement, to landings on both feet. These complex movements involve basic attributes of balance, arm-leg coordination, leg muscle power. Thus, the inability to jump well may be caused by deficits of more than one kind.

Chart 5

AGE (In months)	BEHAVIOR
0–1	Raises chin, lateral head movements.
$2\frac{1}{2}$	Pushes up with arms while lying on stomach.
$5\frac{1}{2}$	Sits alone momentarily.
7	Sits alone steadily.
9	Creeps.
$10\frac{1}{2}$	Walks when led, making stepping movements.
13	Stands alone.
$13\frac{1}{2}$–$14\frac{1}{2}$	Walks alone.

Chart 6

Complex Locomotor Activities

AGE (In years-months)	BEHAVIOR
1	
2	May walk sideways or backwards.
3	May walk on tip-toes, able to walk in straight lines.
3	May walk 1-inch line, for 10 feet without walking off.
4	Run, stop, start, turn. Walking rate stabilizes (about 170 per minute)
5	Skilled running, with proper arm action, galloping.
6	Skipping.

Chart 7

Jumping

AGE (In years-months)	JUMPING BEHAVIOR
1.6	Steps off height with one foot; momentarily suspended in air.
2	Beginning of double take-off.
2.6	Good double take-off.
3	Standing broad jump with minimal arm action.
4.6	Some skill in high jumping; able to clear 10 inch barrier.
5–6	Jumping using arm movements; can broad jump a distance of 30 to 40 inches.

Chart 8

AGE (In years-months)	PERCENT OF AGE GROUP WHEN SUCCESSFULLY PERFORMING THE HOPPING PATTERNS*		
	3/3	2/2	3/2
6	3%	10%	3%
6.6	23%	16%	7%
7	35%	19%	10%
7.6	48%	38%	18%
8	63%	53%	31%

*Hopping patterns: 3 left/3 right; 2 left/2 right; 3 left/2 right.

One test for assessing motor ability requires children to hop alternately from one foot to the other without breaking their rhythmic hopping pattern.[11] A recent study of 200 boys by Keogh and Pedigo[11] established norms for boys on this type of task.

Alternate hopping is dependent upon a number of attributes such as: (a) dynamic balance; (b) the ability to coordinate two sides of the body; (c) the ability to transfer a movement pattern from one side to the other; (d) the ability to perceive a rhythmic pattern. The children were given a visual demonstration of three hopping patterns which were 3/3, 2/2, and 3/2. They scored a passing grade: (a) if they made a smooth transition from one foot to the other with little or no delay; (b) if only one foot touched the ground at a time. It is uncertain what scores might be obtained from girls in this type of task.

It is apparent from the data that not until they are eight years old could the majority of boys successfully accomplish even one of these kinds of tasks. At the age of five years, 90 per cent or more of the boys surveyed were unable to perform the patterns. The most difficult combination for the boys was the unequal 3/2 sequence.

Chart 9 combines some of the measures from previous charts. Using these norms, a parent or teacher should be able to make a cursory assessment of selected motor behaviors of children.

AVERAGE PERFORMANCES, BY AGE, IN SELECTED PERCEPTUAL-MOTOR TASKS

This section of the chapter presents performance averages derived from a study which was carried out specifically to provide content for this text. Three hundred sixty-five children, ranging in years from four to twelve, were tested in

Chart 9

The Acquisition of Selected Perceptual-Motor
Attributes in Normal Children*

A Summary

AGE (In years-months)	ATTRIBUTES
0.4	Looks at hand and at objects
1	Stand Alone
	Walks alone
2	Walking speed, and rhythm stabilizes
	Walks on tip-toes
	Jumps and lands on both feet
3	Evidences weight shift in throwing, but with no step into throw
	Can walk a line accurately for 10 feet
4	Can catch 16 inch playground ball bounced chest-high to him 4 out of 5 times
	Jumps over 10 inch obstacle
5	Can throw 16 inch playground ball from 10 to 11 feet
6	Broad jumps and runs with good arm action
	Accuracy in left-right discriminations of body and in space
	Can gallop and skip
7	Throws, stepping with foot opposite to throwing arm
8	Alternately hops from one foot to the other with no break in rhythmic pattern
	Can make left-right judgments about another person
9	

*The age at which a majority of normal children evidence the behaviors listed.

a battery composed of five categories of tasks: body-image, general agility, balance, ball interception, and locomotor ability.

The norms for these tasks are presented by age for selected sub-tasks within this total battery. The averages presented offer helpful guidelines for teachers and parents when evaluating the perceptual-motor attributes of children.

Exact procedures for administering these sub-tests are to be found in the Appendix (page 183). Separate norms are presented for boys and girls. In general, it was found that tasks for the balance and gross agility categories differentiate between girls of various ages. The category for locomotor agility, contained tests evaluating two independent attributes, one involving locomotor accuracy, and the other simple locomotor abilities without the need for close visual inspection ($r = .44$). The test in the throwing category employs a ball which may be too large for many childrens' hands. The tests apparently evaluated independent attributes (see correlation matrix, and factor analysis Appendix, page 193); while at the same time each made a substantial contribution to the total battery score.

Care must be taken when interpreting the scores obtained in the body perception category because correct responses in the second level of this category can be the result of chance. If the examiner thinks a child is guessing, this portion of the test should be administered a second time to check the validity of the responses.

The norms for the battery contained in this section are meant to provide guidelines for the evaluation of motor attributes in which the larger muscles of the body are involved. Fine motor coordinations underlying writing may be assessed by referring to material on drawing behavior in Chapter 6.

On the pages which follow, samples of the behavior which relate to the scores indicated are listed. Several charts contain the average scores for a population of children designated as Educationally Handicapped by the Los Angeles City Schools. Thus, when testing a group of individual children, comparisons made between "normal" behavior and performance averages obtained from children who have been identified as evidencing mild to moderate perceptual-motor problems may be carried out.

Body Perception.   Detail instructions for the administration of the body-perception test are given in the Appendix, page 184. Essentially, the child is to demonstrate that he knows where his front, side, and back are, by lying on them when asked to do so. If a child has a mental age above seven, the initial four parts of the test may be omitted, and only the final part of the test may be administered. The final task involves demonstrating that the child knows the relation to objects or persons (lie down with your feet nearest me), and this is followed by a series of tasks involving left-right discriminations, *i.e.,* lie on your left side, (while in a back lying position) "raise your left hand in the air", "raise your left leg", and finally two tasks in which the child is asked to react to more complex directions, and cross his body, touching . . . " . . . your left elbow with your right hand . . " , and finally "touch your right knee with your left hand". Scores from a population of 365 normal children are shown on Chart 10.

Correlation of the scores of the total subjects in this test to the total battery score was .73.

A group of 38 children with minimal to moderate perceptual-motor impairments tested in this portion of the battery achieved scored as shown on Chart 11.

4

Chart 10

Average Scores for 365 Normal Children

AGE (In years)	BEHAVIOR SCORES
4–5	Able to complete first five tasks successfully but unable to make any left-right judgments of body parts better than would be expected by chance.
6	Able to identify accurately left, right arms and legs, but unable to cross body and make complex judgments in final two tasks.
7–11	Children able to make all judgments.

GROSS AGILITY

The second category of the test battery tests the ability to move the body in a coordinated manner, while remaining relatively fixed. Two sub-tasks are scored. The first involves scoring how fast a child can arise from a back-lying position, using both time and form as criteria. The second involves the duplication of a demonstrated four-count movement from standing position, to kneeling, and back to standing: (1) kneel left, (2) kneel right, (3) stand left, (4) stand right. The gross agility score is a combination of scores achieved on each of these two tasks.

Chart 11

AGE	BEHAVIOR
5–8	Could identify planes of the body, front, back, etc., but no left-right identifications better than would be expected by chance.
9–10	Could not identify left and right better than would be expected by chance.
11–12	Could identify left and right hands, etc., but could not cross body, i.e., "touch your left knee with your right hand."
13–16	Could identify left and right, and could make about one-half of judgments requiring movements across the body, i.e., "touch left elbow with right hand."

Chart 12

Gross Agility Scores for Normal Boys*

AGE (In years-months)	AVERAGE SCORES (In years)
4.6	8.5
5.6	9.5
6.6–11.6	9.75

The average scores achieved in the gross agility category by normal subjects are given in Charts 12 and 13. In general, the boys' scores clustered so closely that it was impossible to accurately differentiate between the various age groups. A possible reason for this may rest with measures used in the test, especially the first test (back lying position to a stand) which depends upon leg and trunk power, as well as integrative mechanisms. The mean scores for the girls, when plotted by age, however, show a gradual increase. Thus, the score seems more helpful in rating the girls than in differentiating between levels of performance for normal boys.

Chart 13

Gross Agility Scores for Normal Girls

AGE (In years-months)	AVERAGE SCORES (In years)
5	4.75
5.6–6.6	8.45
7.6	8.75
8.6	9.25
9.6–11.6	9.75

*See scoring methods and test administration in Appendix.

The same tasks were given to a population of 38 children having a range from minimal to moderate perceptual-motor problems. In Chart 14, the mean scores by age represent the combined scores for the boys and girls.

The difference is apparent between the scores achieved by the normal population and those with motor problems. Thus, this test would seem to be a helpful measure to use in differentiating children with motor problems from those who do not.

Correlation between gross agility scores and the total battery score was .48.

BALANCE

The third category of the battery measures static balance. This attribute is evaluated by imposing various stresses upon a child who is asked to posture in an immobile position on one foot. Portions of the test are timed, and, in addition, the child is asked to: (*a*) stand with arms folded, (*b*) his eyes closed, (*c*) to posture on his non-preferred foot with the above restrictions. The balance score was found to be predictive of the total battery score in data collected in a previous study using children with minimal to moderate perceptual-motor problems (r = .82).

Chart 15 represents the average scores achieved by a population of normal children. The scores are separated by sex, when sex differences were significant in the data.

This same test was administered to children with mild to moderate perceptual-motor problems. Again the performance scores for the normal population differed significantly from those of the children with motor problems. In Chart 16, the scores for the boys and girls are combined. Again, the differences between normal performance and the performance of children with motor problems is apparent.

Chart 14

Combined Scores for Boys and Girls in Gross Agility

(POPULATION RANGE—FROM MINIMAL TO MODERATE
PERCEPTUAL-MOTOR PROBLEMS)

AGE (In years)	AVERAGE SCORE (In years)
5–8	2.6
9–10	5.9
11–12	8.6
13–16	8.5

Chart 15

Balance Scores for Normal Population of Boys and Girls

AVERAGE SCORE AND AGE (In years-months)	SEX	BEHAVIOR
4.6–5	Girls	Could balance on preferred foot with arms folded for 3 to 4 seconds, eyes open, but seldom for 10 seconds.
4.6–5	Boys	Could balance on preferred foot with arms folded for 10 seconds; unable to balance on preferred foot with eyes closed for 5 seconds.
5.6–6	Girls	Could balance on preferred foot with eyes open for 10 seconds.
5.6–6	Boys	Could balance on preferred foot with eyes closed, and assisted by arms for 5 seconds.
6.6–7	Girls	Could balance on preferred foot with eyes closed and assisted by arms for 5 seconds.
6.6–7	Boys	Could balance on preferred foot with eyes closed, arms folded, for 5 seconds.
7.6–8.6	Boys and Girls	Able to balance on preferred foot with arms folded for 5 seconds.
9–11.6	Boys and Girls	Able to posture on non-preferred foot assisted by arms, with eyes closed, for 5 seconds.

Chart 16

Balance Scores for 38 Boys and Girls with Motor Problems

AGE (In years)	SEX	BEHAVIOR
5–8	Boys and Girls	Could balance on preferred foot, eyes open, using arms for 2 to 6 seconds.
9–10	Boys and Girls	Could balance on preferred foot, eyes open, using arms for 5 seconds.
11–16	Boys and Girls	Could balance on preferred foot, eyes closed, arms folded, for 5 seconds.

LOCOMOTOR ABILITY

The first level tasks within this category involve: crawling, walking, hopping, and jumping forward and backward three or more times. If the subject completes the five tasks, using the coordination essential to performing the tasks, his total score is 5, 1 for each task.

The second level tasks require a child to jump and then hop with accuracy into twelve squares (1 x 1 foot) inscribed on a mat. There are six squares in each of two parallel rows.

Chart 17 records the average scores by age and sex of the normal population surveyed.

The same locomotor agility test was administered to a population of children with minimal perceptual-motor problems. Chart 18 records the combined scores of the boys and girls in this group.

Chart 17

Locomotor Agility for Normal Population

AGE (In years-months)	SEX	AVERAGE SCORES
4.6–5	Girls	Able to perform the five tasks but not with accuracy within the squares.
4.6–5	Boys	Able to crawl, walk, jump forward; unable to jump backward or to hop for three consecutive times.
5.6–6.6	Girls	Able to jump forward with accuracy into the squares; had difficulty jumping diagonally into alternate squares in each row; unable to hop or jump backwards with accuracy into the squares.
5.6–6	Boys	Able to execute the five tasks; had difficulty performing the tasks with accuracy into the squares.
7–7.6	Girls	Able to jump accurately diagonally into alternate squares in each row; had difficulty jumping backward with accuracy into the squares.
6.6–8	Boys	Able to jump accurately diagonally into alternate squares in each row; unable to jump backward with accuracy into the squares.
8.6–11.6	Boys and Girls	Able to hop in a row of six squares; had difficulty hopping diagonally into alternate squares in each row.

Chart 18

Locomotor Agility for 38 Children With
Perceptual-Motor Problems

AGE (In years)	SEX	AVERAGE SCORE
5–9	Boys and Girls	Unable to jump or to hop, but inaccurately.
9–16	Boys and Girls	Able to jump in a row of six squares straight ahead; unable to jump diagonally into alternate squares.

It is apparent from the data we have collected that neurologically impaired children can often hop and jump reasonably well, but when asked to do so with accuracy (into squares over lines) with good visual control of their movements, they fail to do well. Correlation between locomotor agility score and total battery was .75.

Intercepting Balls. This test consists of two sub-tasks: the first requires the child to catch a 16 inch playground ball, bounced once from a distance of 15 feet away, so that it rebounds chest-high to the child. The score for this is one point for each of the 5 trials. The second sub-test requires the child to touch with his index finger a softball swung on a string (15 inches long) in a 180 degree arc, at arms distance away from the subject. The ball must be touched before it swings three times. The score is one point for each of the five trials. The score for the total test is 10 points (norms are shown on Chart 19, page 40).

A critical time in a child's life occurs when he is five and ready for kindergarten. As he begins school, he should be evaluated to discover, as early as possible, any deficits he may have in his perceptual-motor functioning.

Based on the data described in this chapter, several criteria are suggested as a guide to evaluating five- and seven-year-old children. If deficits are discovered, a child should be referred to specialists for a thorough evaluation, so that a remedial program can be developed.

SUMMARY

The reader may utilize the previous norms in a number of ways. Using the battery of tests found in the Appendix, he may survey in rather exact parameters a population of children with whom he is dealing. At the same time, less precise check-sheets may be developed upon inspection of the previous pages, which would enable the expeditious survey of a large population of children within a relatively short period of time. It has thus been attempted in this chapter and in the section dealing with drawing, to present a "cafeteria" of tests and norms from

Chart 19

Ball Interception for Normal Population

AGE (In years-months)	SEX	SCORES
4.6–5	Girls	Caught ball 2 out of 5 trials; unable to touch swinging ball.
4.6–5	Boys	Caught ball 2 out of 5 trials; unable to touch swinging ball.
5.6–6	Boys and Girls	Caught ball _____ trials; unable to touch swinging ball.
6.6–7	Boys and Girls	Caught ball 5 out of 5 trials; able to touch swinging ball 2 out of 5 trials.
7.6–8	Girls	Caught ball 5 out of 5 trials; able to touch swinging ball 3 out of 5 trials.
7.6–11.5	Boys	Caught ball 5 out of 5 trials; able to touch swinging ball 3 out of 5 trials.
8.6–11.5	Girls	Caught ball 5 out of 5 trials; able to touch swinging ball 4 out of 5 trials.

Chart 20

Evaluation Criteria for a Four-Year-Old Child

A four-year-old child should be able to:

1. Walk perfectly, changing speed, and evidence a consistent walking speed and rhythm.
2. Balance on one foot with eyes open for 4 seconds or more.
3. Take three jumping steps forward.
4. Jump off a 2 foot high obstacle, and broad jump 2 feet forward from a standing position.
5. Throw a small ball 10 to 15 feet.

Chart 21

Evaluation Criteria for a Five-Year-Old Child

A five year old child should be able:

1. to balance on his preferred foot, with eyes open, with arms folded, for at least four seconds.
2. to catch a 16 inch rubber ball bounced chest high from distance of 15 feet, 4 out of 5 times.
3. to jump forward and to hop forward on one foot three consecutive times.
4. to identify body parts, limbs, front, back and sides.
5. to run in a coordinated manner, with integration of arms and legs.
6. to jump over a 10 inch high barrier.

It is *unlikely* that a five year old will be able:

1. to identify his left and right body parts better than would be expected by chance (*i.e.*, better than 75% correct responses).
2. to alternately hop from foot to foot, without undue hesitation or placing both feet on the ground simultaneously, in either a 1/2, 3/3, or 2/3 pattern.
3. to touch a ball swinging on a 15 inch string through a 180 degree arc, arms distance away.
4. to jump or hop with accuracy into small squares.

which the teacher, parent, or administrator may select according to their needs. Furthermore, certain attributes are indicative of a number of gross motor attributes, and thus additional time may be saved if only they are assessed. For example, the balance test described is usually highly correlated with a number of gross motor attributes including agility and the like.

CHART 22

Evaluation Criteria for A Seven-Year-Old Child

By the time a seven-year-old child is in second grade, he should be able to:

1. Make all types of left-right identifications of his body parts, body movements, and body-to-object relationships (place the box nearest your left side).
2. Throw a ball with proper step (*i.e.*, using foot opposite to his throwing arm) and weight shift.
3. Get up from a back lying position to a standing position in 1 to 1.5 seconds.
4. Balance on one foot with eyes closed for 5 seconds.
5. Skip, gallop, and run in a coordinated manner (frequently cultural expectations will "corrupt" this performance . . . *i.e.*, boys prefer to gallop).

It is also considered advisable if the measures of gross body agility presented in this chapter are combined with others assessing fine motor ability. Thus the reader should consult norms for writing and drawing behavior presented in Chapter 6 when devising a battery of tests with which to survey a population of normal or atypical children.

REFERENCES

1. Adams, N. and Caldwell, W.: "The Children's Somatic Apperception Test," *J. Genet. Psych.: 68:* 43–57, 1963.
2. Belmont, L. and Brich, H. G.: "Lateral Dominance and Left-Right Awareness In Normal Children," *Child. Dev.: 34:* 257–270, 1963.
3. Benton, Arthur L.: *Right-Left Discrimination and Finger Localization,* New York, Hoeber, 14, 1959.
4. Berges, J. and Lezine, L.: *The Imitation of Gestures,* (translated by Arthur H. Parmelee) The Spastics Society Medical Education and Information Unit Association, London, William Heinemann, Medical Books Ltd., 1965.
5. Cratty, Bryant J.: *The Perceptual-Motor Attributes of Mentally Retarded Children and Youth,* (Monograph), Los Angeles County Mental Retardation Services Board, 1966.
6. Espenschade, Anna S. and Eckert, Helen M.: *Motor Development,* Columbus, Ohio, Charles E. Merrill Books, Inc., 1967.
7. Gesell, A. and Thompson, H.: *Infant Behavior: Its Genesis and Growth,* New York, McGraw-Hill Book Co., 1934.
8. Halverson, H. M.: "An Experimental Study of Prehension In Infants By Means of Systematic Cinema Records," *Gent. Psych. Mono.: 10:* 107–286, 1931.
9. Hill, S. D., McCullum, A. A. and Sceau, A.: "Relation of Training in Motor Activity to Development of Left-Right Directionality in Mentally Retarded Children: Exploratory Study," *Percept. & Mot. Skills: 24:* 363–366, 1967.
10. Ilg, Frances L. and Ames, Louise Bates: *School Readiness,* New York, Harper & Row, 1965.
11. Keogh, Jack F. and Pedigo, P.: "An Evaluation of Performance On Rhythmic Hopping Patterns," Sponsored by the National Institute of Child Health and Human Development (Grant HD 09059-03), UCLA, 1967. (Unpublished).
12. McGraw, Myrtle B.: *The Neuromuscular Maturation of the Human Infant,* New York, Hafner Publishing Co., 1966.
13. Piaget, J.: *The Origins of Intelligence in Children,* New York: International University Press, 103–107, 1952.
14. Shirley, M. M.: *The First Two Years: A Study of Twenty-Five Babies. Vol. I. Postural and Locomotor Development,* Minneapolis, University of Minnesota Press, 1931.
15. Swenson, C. H.: "Empirical Evaluation of Human Figure Drawings," *Psychol. Bull.: 54:* 431–466, 1954.
16. Uzgiris, Ina C.: "Ordinality in the Development of Schemas For Relating To Objects, In *Exceptional Infant Vol. 1,* Jerome Hellmuth (Ed.), Washington: Special Child Publications, 315–334, 1967.
17. White, Burton L. and Held, Richard: "Plasticity of Sensori-motor Development in the Human Infant," In *The Causes of Behavior: Readings in Child Development and Educational Psychology,* Judy F. Rosenblith and Wesley Allinsmith (Eds.), Boston: Allyn & Bacon, 1966.
18. Wild, Monica R.: "The Behavior Pattern of Throwing and Some Observations Concerning Its Course of Development in Children," *Res. Quart.: 9-3:* 20–24, 1938.

4

Principles of
Perceptual-Motor Education

INTRODUCTION

An initial question that must be resolved when attempting to integrate special programs involving movement into the total educational program is to determine which children should be involved. This question derives its importance from the literature reviewed in Chapter 2 which reveals that special programs of movement education inserted into school programs will not help *all* children learn better. Only between 6 to 15 per cent of the children within a normal population will usually evidence the need for special movement education classes. It is believed that the information in Chapter 3, dealing with various indices of perceptual-motor behavior evidenced by normal children, should aid in this initial screening.

Hopefully within the next several years, most elementary schools in the country will begin to identify children with movement problems and will provide them with special motor education classes 2 or 3 times a week. Such classes should focus on the improvement of large muscle control as well as upon visual control of hand movements.

It is not unusual to find that children with mild to moderate perceptual-motor problems will evidence other kinds of behavioral deficits. For instance, their speech may be poor, their vision may not be acute, and/or they will have problems in reading, writing, arithmetic, and spelling.

The parents of such a child usually have important decisions to make in determining the type and amount of therapy that is needed. The answers to these questions are not simple; they hinge upon the income of the parent, the type of difficulties encountered by the child, the nature of the diagnosis, and the evaluator.

More basic questions underlie *these,* including just how much transfer will occur between the attributes designated improvable within the various therapies involved. It is believed that three primary guidelines are helpful when arriving at decisions of this nature.

(1) The child should, if possible, receive as comprehensive an evaluation as possible, including assessment of physical status, ocular functioning, emotional health, subject matter competencies, perceptual-motor functioning, and auditory perception.

(2) At times parents should exercise their own judgment, because they are in the best position to observe on a daily basis the nature of their child's problems. However, parents should be watchful so that concern for their child's welfare does not blind them to the nature and the severeity of the problems he may exhibit.

Parents should seek the advice of a competent professional partner, their doctor, or a psychologist to serve as a coordinator for their child's remedial program. By having a trustworthy professional "coordinator," two errors can be avoided. The professional partner will restrain conscientious parents from exhausting themselves and the child by dashing about to too many therapy sessions each week. Also, frequent professional guidance will protect parents from the occasional unscrupulous person who might take advantage of them.

Any kind of special training in movement should be considered within a total context of remedial help for children with various kinds of learning, behavioral, sensory, and motor problems. To expect motor training to exert magical influences upon a variety of learning, sensory, and/or communication disorders is unrealistic, and parents and teachers basing their hopes on this hypothesis will usually be disappointed.

GENERAL SKILLS VERSUS SPECIFIC
MOTOR TRAINING

Another important question to be answered involves the proposition of time of a child's program which should be devoted to activities strengthening basic perceptual-motor attributes and the amount of time which should be devoted to teaching specific skills. For example, should the entire period be taken up with balance and agility tasks of a general nature or should time be used in teaching specific skills needed for a particular game; should basic hand-eye coordination drills using the chalk board be employed for the total period or should the child be taught to form the letters used in handwriting?

Programs of exploratory creative movement permeates the educational programs of many European countries. These programs, intended to enhance general motor attributes, creative energies, and similar qualities in children, are advanced by their proponents who believe that these programs form the base for the later efficient use of the body in sports skills and dance movements.

The research suggests that general types of movement activities are most beneficial during the early years of a child's education program, but that as he matures, more emphasis should be placed on exact procedures for executing specific skills. It seems that if general programs of movement improvement are continued too long, the child will not acquire skills prized by his peer group. However, if a child is exposed too early to only specific skills, his ability to move well in a variety of life's activities may not fully develop. A child with movement problems, however, may be exposed to activities intended to build basic attributes for a longer period of time each day and for several years beyond the age during which such a program should be continued with a normal child.

There is, of course, an overlapping between activities aimed at improving basic attributes and those found in specific sports. However, the literature does not support the assumption that a great deal of transfer occurs between various sports movements which appear to be alike.[2,11] For instance, badminton skills may not aid tennis skills. At the same time, transfer may occur between tasks intended to help improve basic movement attributes. A recent study, for example, found that practicing various seated balances aided standing balance.[13]

Thus, an accurate answer to the question whether basic movement attributes or skill specifics should be concentrated upon hinges on research dealing with the nature of transfer of training, on research outlining the parameters of motor performance itself, on the age of the child involved, as well as on the degree of motor ineptitude evidenced within a given group of children.

It was, therefore, with some apprehension that the following chart was prepared. In general, it suggests that, during the earlier years of a child's life, basic movement attributes should be concentrated upon such as: balance, agility, hand-eye movements, rhythm, ball handling, and locomotor movement. As the child reaches middle and late childhood, however, increased attention should be paid to channeling and molding these general attributes into specific movement patterns demanded in the classroom and on the playfield.

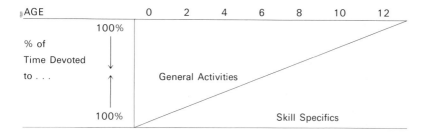

PRINCIPLES OF LEARNING

Sound learning principles should be incorporated into a program of perceptual-motor education just as they should underlie every component of educational programs. Attention should be paid to the length of the practice session, the amount of rest given between practice session, the nature of the learning cues available to the child, the distractions present in the learning environment, and the amount of space in which the activities are held. Further, care should be taken to motivate children to work to optimum levels.

The principles of learning which follow summarize those presented in other texts dealing with motor learning written by Cratty.[2,4]*

1. Practice sessions should be separated by adequate rest periods. The longer and more strenuous the practice session, the longer the rest periods. Children will practice tasks which hold their interest because of their novelty or complexity with

---

*For a more thorough review and research support of these principles, the reader is referred to other references by Oxendine[10] and Singer.[11]

relatively little rest between trials. However, when the instructor notices that this interest is waning, rest periods of increased duration should be instituted.

2. There is an optimum duration of practice sessions for the development of any given skill. It has been found, for example, that twenty minutes a day is sometimes optimum for the teaching of handwriting.

3. More satisfaction occurs when learning a skill quickly. Learning is expedited when as much of an activity is presented to the learner as he is capable of acquiring at a given time. The usual practice, when the skill has to be broken down for easier assimilation, is to provide progressive-part practice. In this method, an initial part of the skill is learned, then a second part. These two parts are then combined and practiced. After they have been practiced, a third part is learned and added to the earlier parts. Then the three parts are practiced together. This procedure continues until the whole complex skill is assimilated.

4. Care must be taken not to "over-teach" a skill. Children with learning problems cannot organize a barrage of sensory information provided by the instructor, by the nature of the task, and/or by movement feedback from initial practice attempts. While it is more important to insert instruction during the initial stages of learning, it should be kept in mind that too much information may block the "channel capacity" of a learner making it difficult for him to acquire a skill or understand the type of movement he is to engage in.

A variety of methods for gaining sensory information should be provided a learner at the appropriate time and in reasonable amounts. For example, children with visual-perceptual problems are likely to be helped very little by a demonstration, whereas they would derive more benefit from a careful verbal explanation of a movement, accompanied with manual guidance. After they have acquired the general movement pattern desired, it then may be more advantageous to them to make the final adjustments in their neuromotor system by self-direction.

5. Up to a point, retention is increased by over-learning a given skill. Over-learning, by approximately 150 per cent in excess of a given criteria, is usually best.

6. The learning of skills is increased when the learner understands, prior to the learning situation, he will be required to remember the skill and repeat it at a later time. Retention is also heightened if the learner is informed of the exact reason for practicing the task.

7. Retention of rhythmic movements having internal consistency is more enduring than retention of unrelated movements in a series.

HOW DOES TRANSFER OCCUR?
WHAT TRANSFERS?

Transfer may be defined as the influence of one task upon the learning or performance of a second. When designing a program of perceptual-motor education, one must determine how best to elicite desirable transfer. The literature on this topic suggests that transfer must be provided for in the manner in which the tasks are taught and related.[6] Several considerations must also be kept in mind when teaching for transfer of training.

1. Practice of a number of related tasks is more likely to elicit transfer to another task than the practice of only one task. Therefore, if improved balance is

desired, a number of balance tasks should be practiced, including dynamic balance using balance beams and static balance. Also, for a group of children to realize and act upon the fact that space can be ordered in left-right dimensions, they must engage in many left-right activities.

2. "Cognitive bridges" must be built between two tasks to elicit maximum transfer. To accomplish this, a child with movement problems should be informed of this improvement transfer to improvement in self-concept is desired and expected. Also, the reasons for a drill should be explained, keeping the explanation within the child's limits of understanding, if the drill is to have a maximum effect upon a basic movement attribute, on a more complex skill, or on the execution of a game. Moreover, performance in complex tasks may often be greater if components of the task are practiced.

3. In children who are less able in motor skills, more transfer between various activities, if the above principles are followed, may be expected to occur than between tasks practiced by children free from motor deficits.

In addition to these general considerations, principles more closely related to the improvement of motor attributes should also be followed.

SIMULTANEOUS EDUCATION OF MORE THAN ONE ATTRIBUTE

When designing movement tasks for any given attribute, it is possible to incorporate more than one attribute in the task. For example, improvement of agility with tumbling-like movements, rolling and falling, can be combined with body-image training. In other words, the child may be asked to pause as he rolls down a mat and state whether he is on his left or right side. Further, when learning to fall, he may be asked to fall on his left or right side. Also, if a child is walking a balance beam, he may be asked to step off on one side and then on the other and state whether it is his left or right foot that has touched the ground. Again, if a child is asked to balance on a small unstable platform to improve balance, he may be asked to play catch with another child balanced in a similar way, thereby incorporating balance training and training in ball-handling skill. Further, a series of line walking tasks may aid a child expand his ability to remember things in a series and aid dynamic balance.

Actually only a small number of activities may be needed to favorably alter several attributes. Most ball games incorporate agility, locomotor movements, and ball-handling. However, children with more marked motor problems, those who are mentally less capable, or those who are immature may need a variety of simple activities designed to improve a single attribute.

SEQUENCING ACTIVITIES

While it is desirable to be creative when devising activities within a perceptual-motor education program, it is equally important to keep in mind sequences of two kinds when working with children in such a context. First in importance is the need to consider carefully the order of difficulty of tasks to which the child is exposed. For the activity to be productive, the tasks must be made as simple as possible when working with children who have motor problems. Failure to do so can create problems such as one teacher in special education experienced. The teacher was attempting to improve the balance of a group of five-year-old children who were severely retarded and who had severe motor problems combined with hyperactivity. The children were instructed to walk a balance beam (4 inches wide; 6 inches high) while keeping their eyes on a mark on the wall located at the end of the beam!

The task was impossible for this group of children to accomplish. They needed simple tasks of practice in walking lines painted on the floor at least 6 inches wide and in performing simple static balances on mats. Furthermore, playing left-right "body-image" games with children whose mental ages are much below six will also prove frustrating both to the ambitious teacher and to her pupils.

The teacher should be aware of normative data so that she can determine where in a sequence her particular group of children with their unique mental and motor attributes should begin their training. Secondly, the teacher should be aware of the ways in which balance, agility, and body-image can be fragmented into sub-tasks. To help the teacher, normative data concerning various perceptual-motor tasks are contained in Chapter 3 and texts by Cratty,[5] Mosston,[9] and others.

SELF-CONTROL, DECISION MAKING

Children with perceptual-motor problems usually feel more secure if initially a reasonably "tight" structure is provided in the learning environment. The teacher, cognizant of this, should give exact initial directions during his first contacts with the students. Later, when the children seem able to remove some of the structure imposed upon them, the degree of structuring can be lessened. The extent to which the children can assume responsibility for making some of the decisions inherent in the learning situation will determine the amount of structure needed. This shift of decision making from the teacher to the children should be accomplished gradually and sequentially. The shifting of emphasis from the teacher to the learner should occur when the children demonstrate their ability to control themselves and their own activities. Writers in physical education[8] and in business theory[12] have described in some detail how teacher-centered instruction (or boss-centered supervision) can gradually and purposefully evolve into group-centered direction.

When some degree of decision making is assumed by the learners, more intense, highly motivated, and purposeful learning will occur. For example, after giving children a task (*i.e.,* different ways to walk a line), they may be asked to demonstrate four ways to walk the line. Later on, a decision concerning the frequency of the task can be transferred to the child by asking him to walk the line in as many ways as possible. The teacher in this situation still retains most of the decisions for himself, including those governing the time (now), and the location (where), what kind of task (balance beam walking), and evaluation methods (the instructor's reinforcing remarks).

Tannenbaum and Schmidt[12] suggest that effective supervisors in business institutions carefully examine the forces in the group, the forces in the situation, and the forces within themselves before deciding upon the amount of authority or the amount of group-centered decisions which will result in the most effective performance. Teachers of children with movement problems can benefit from these suggestions. After an examination of all variables, a teacher might then be able to determine if his personal needs for authority and control prevent him from effectively transferring decision-making to his students when appropriate. Further, the teacher who simply removes structure without being sensitive to the students' ability to assume the responsibility of making decisions will soon realize his mistake when the class is beyond his control.

Helpful ways of assessing the children's ability to maintain self-control are contained in the activities listed in Chapter 5. One means of assessment is the determination of the child's ability to inhibit the speed of his movements. If he can exercise this control, usually he is ready to make choices about task performance modifications.

Practicing the techniques outlined in Chapter 5 should better prepare children to place themselves under their own control, and should help them structure in certain components of their learning environment. The importance for decision making on the part of the students is derived from several highly respected learning theorists[1] who have suggested that no true learning takes place unless the learners are involved in decisions about the learning process. The teacher of perceptual-motor skills finds himself in an excellent position to encourage problem solving behavior at various levels of sophistication in motor tasks, when he begins to allow time within his lesson for children to think about what they are doing instead of continually providing such information himself.

INTEGRATION AND DIFFERENTIATION OF BODY-PARTS

The need for a child to control his general level of arousal and excitation is stated in Chapter 5. This section points out an equally important need for a child to control, in specific ways, tensions and levels of activation in specific body parts. This is important because it is not unusual to see children with perceptual-motor problems evidence inappropriate "spill-overs" of muscular tensions from one body part to another. For instance, if such a child is asked to touch sequentially the fingers of one hand to the thumb, the other hand will often evidence "twitchings" reflecting similar movements. Moreover, as some children concentrate upon writing with one hand, the other hand will be inordinately tense or too relaxed and consequently may not hold the paper on the table or desk appropriately.

In addition to the inability to localize specific energies in portions of the body when called for in given tasks, the child with motor problems may be unable to integrate various body parts with one another. He may not step appropriately (See Chapter 3, page 30) with his feet as he throws with his hands. Moreover, a "jumping-jack" exercise may not be performed in a coordinated manner. When executing the jump, his arms may "flop" at his side or be lifted ahead of the leg thrust.

5

Therefore, basic to a program of perceptual-motor training are the activities designed to develop the differentiation and integration of body parts. Some such as the activities suggested in Chapter 8, involve the trampoline. In this activity, jumping jacks performed as the child leaves the resiliant bed of the trampoline increase the time permitted for him to integrate movements of arms and legs.

Also, an uncoordinated child may be unable to transfer a rhythmic pattern from one side of his body to the other (See Chapter 3, page 31 for norms). As he may also evidence the inability to integrate his upper limbs with his lower limbs, it often appears as if the child's nervous system is somehow bisected at the waist and down the middle of his body. Coordination may be defined as the integration of the orchestra of "muscle-instruments" into a pleasing symphony of movements. Every effort should be made to help the coordinated child play his "concerto" in tune and reduce the dissonance usually observed as they attempt various complex action patterns.

VISUAL MOTOR INTEGRATION AND BREAKDOWN

It is invariably found that children with movement problems are unable to integrate movement with vision; they are unable to make accurate movements with their upper limbs and with their body under good visual control. A chapter has been devoted to techniques which will increase this general attribute. However, if may be appropriate at times to help children become less dependent upon visual monitoring when moving. While at times, it is helpful for a child to pair his vision and movements, and at other times, it may be more advantageous to provide activities which will tend to *separate* the operation of these two systems. Walking provides an excellent example to illustrate this point. When first learning to walk, a child coordinates his movements by watching each step. Between the second and third year, the normal child no.longer has to watch each footstep, in fact to do so seems to inhibit his progress. A child with movement problems, however, may continue to spend too much time observing foot placement while walking, which tends to make him less efficient in getting around in his environment. Furthermore, he finds it safer to watch where he is going instead of concentrating on the means of locomotion.

When walking balance beams, or when walking lines, the child may watch targets placed in various relationships to his line of walk. Drawing with the eyes closed as well as with them open may help free a child's movements from un-needed control by his visual system.

Getman[7] suggests many ways in which movement and vision may be paired, beginning with simple head movements accompanied by target fixation. Scores obtained on movement tasks in which little visual control is needed (hopping, jumping, etc.) are not correlated with scores obtained from the same task in which accuracy, and thus closer visual inspection, is required (*i.e.,* "Hop into those squares like this"). When requiring close and accurate pairing of vision and movement, a separate and important attribute is being enhanced. It is possible that motor education programs may be helpful primarily for the visual training given the participants as they are required to watch their own moving body parts!

SOCIAL COMPLEXITY

The degree of social pressure a child feels when performing greatly influences his performance. Indeed, a task performed alone usually becomes an entirely different experience for a child when he is required to perform in front of a group. Some of the subtle and obvious ways in which the social context influences individual performance of motor skills are described by Cratty.[3]

It is important when working with children who have motor skill problems initially to provide situations which are free of social pressures and sanctions. One of the primary advantages of a special program of motor education is this release from competitive and social pressures.

After a child becomes capable of performing in a situation which is relatively free of social tensions, the instructor may then add "pressure" by gradually increasing the number in the group. First, a single observing friend may be brought in to watch the performance of a task (*i.e.,* handwriting), thus conditioning the child to minimum stress. Later, other children may be added gradually to the group and be required to write at the same time the first child writes.

Most children with average intelligence who have coordination problems are quickly made aware of these problems by their peer group. Punishment meted out by the peer group adds to coordination problems as tensions further interfere with muscular accuracy. Some of this emotional "overlay" consisting of interfering muscular tensions may be alleviated by the removal of the caustic bystanders. However, this cannot always be accomplished since most motor performances (writing and playing games) are frequently carried out in the presence of others. Although many teachers will find it relatively easy to instruct children on an individual basis, little transfer may be found to occur when the child is returned to the disrupting social context which initially contributed to his problem. Thus, a gradual re-introduction of social pressures should take place as increased proficiency in performance is attained.

SCHEDULES AND THE ORGANIZATION OF A PRACTICE SESSION

In addition to the subtle principles outlined in this chapter, there are operational aspects to a program of perceptual-motor education. What should be the length of a single practice session? How frequently during the week should a child practice? The optimum seems to be a three day a week program, Monday–Wednesday–Friday, in which activities are designed to emphasize large muscle movement. The alternate days, Tuesday–Thursday–Saturday, may be taken up with manual tasks such as writing.

The optimum duration of a given practice period will depend upon a number of variables. One hour, separated into 2 thirty-minute periods, or 3 twenty-minute periods-per-day is probably best. Each period should begin with general stretching, agility, balance, and body-image activities, with more vigorous games bringing the period to a close. The final few minutes might be devoted to three or four fitness exercises. The exercises in the program at University of California, at Los Angeles generally consist of two for the shoulder-arm region (a pushing exercise and one which involves the arms and upper back, a pulling movement of some kind), and one for the lower back (some kind of extension movement), and one for the abdominals (bent-leg sit-up). Exercises of this nature exert a remarkably positive effect upon the musculature in these regions, while the general program preceding these exercises build general trunk strength, leg power, and endurance.

SUMMARY

Several primary principles should underlie a program of perceptual-motor education for children with skill problems. Requisite to any program is a thorough and comprehensive evaluation of the emotional, social, educational, perceptual, and motor functioning of the child. Following this type of evaluation, professional advice should be sought concerning just how participation in a program of motor activities may aid in the child's total development.

When working with a child through movement, the educator should engage in activities encouraging the development of basic motor attributes, balance, agility, and the like, as well as in the teaching of specific sport skills and drawing and writing tasks. The child should be exposed to motor activities which will aid him to place himself better under his own control, and when possible, should be permitted to assume some of the structure and decision making within the learning environment.

Activities which aid the child to integrate body parts, as well as those which improve his ability to focus tension in specific body parts should be incorporated into his program. The social complexity of the situation in which he performs should be gradually increased, as he becomes able to perform under increasing degrees of social stress.

Sound learning principles should be followed, including those governing the practice schedule, transfer of training, and motivation. When possible, the child should be encouraged to acquire as much of the whole skill as he is capable of attaining.

REFERENCES

1. Bruner, Jerome: "The Act of Discovery," *Harvard Educational Review: 31:* 21–32: 1961.
2. Cratty, B. J.: *Movement Behavior and Motor Learning,* 2nd Ed., Philadelphia, Lea & Febiger, 1967.
3. ———: *Social Dimensions of Physical Activity,* Englewood Cliffs, New Jersey, Prentice-Hall Inc., 1967.
4. ———: *Psychology and Physical Activity,* Englewood Cliffs, New Jersey, Prentice-Hall Inc., 1968.
5. ———: *Developmental Sequences of Perceptual-Motor Tasks,* Freeport, L.I., New York, Educational Activities, Inc., 1967.
6. Ellis, Henry: *The Transfer of Learning,* New York, The Macmillan Co., 1965.
7. Getman, G. N. and Kane, E. R.: *The Physiology of Readiness,* Minneapolis, Minnesota P.A.S.S. Publishing Co., 1963.
8. Mosston, Muska: *Teaching Physical Education,* Columbus, Ohio, Charles E. Merrill Co., 1966.

9. ———: *Developmental Movement,* Columbus, Ohio, Charles E. Merrill Co., 1965.
10. Oxendine, J. B.: *Psychology of Motor Learning,* New York, Appleton-Century-Crofts, 1968.
11. Singer, Robert: *Motor Learning and Human Performance,* New York, The Macmillan Co., 1968.
12. Tannenbaum, R. and Schmidt, W. H.: "How to Choose a Leadership Pattern," *Harvard Business Review: 36:* 96–100: 1958.
13. Vincent, William: "Transfer Effects Between Motor Skills Judged Similar in Perceptual Components," Unpublished Ed.D. Dissertation, University of California, Los Angeles, 1966.

5

The Adjustment of Arousal Level and the Improvement of Attention

It is not uncommon to find among children with perceptual-motor problems a large number who are hyperactive. It is also true that excessive activity is an impediment to learning. Zeaman and House have suggested that one of the primary contributing factors to learning problems is the inability to focus attention on various tasks.[11]

Their research analyzed the learning in visual discrimination tasks among various groups of children and found that the primary factor differentiating between I.Q. sub-groups within their populations was the inability to even begin to focus on the task. The brighter children began to learn the tasks immediately, while children with lower I.Q.'s were producing learning curves characterized by initial trials during which apparently no learning was taking place, because of a failure to attend to the task.

Ounsted, among others, has found that the I.Q. of hyper-active children is generally lower than in children who are more self-controlled.[9] In studies carried out with normal children, high correlations have been obtained between I.Q. and scores in tasks in which motor control is called for (i.e., "walk as slowly as you can from here to there").[8] Harrison attempted to determine whether he could exert a causal effect upon learning by incorporating training intended to reduce the arousal level of a group of children. His positive findings suggest that indeed specific kinds of activities designed to help children achieve and maintain self-control would be helpful within educational programs for children with learning difficulties.[2]

A number of measures have been utilized to evaluate the activity level of children; direct observation and scoring the duration of time a child is in motion, measuring the amount of free movement engaged in within a prescribed area using electronic scoring techniques (pressure plates in the floor, light beams crossing the room), and various "figetometers" in which slight movement in chairs or while standing on platforms is recorded.[1, 10]

In general, it is found that the singular concept of activity level is in reality composed of several factors[1,11] including apparently purposeful movement related to objects and/or people, behavior which is not goal centered and random rhythmic movements which may be classified as self-stimulation (rocking movements and the like). Thus to help a child place himself under better control, techniques in which a variety of activities may be affected should be engaged in. A number of causes for hyperactivity in children have been postulated.[1] Some have suggested that a child who is hyperactive is evidencing the persistence of an immature stage of development in which the need to manually inspect objects and people is continuing to be evidenced. Others have hypothesized that hyperactivity is a kind of neuromotor "spill-over" from some manfunction in one of the several stages within the perceptual-integration-motor process. A third cause which has been advanced for hyperactivity is that it is evidence of some kind of problem within the child's selection-rejection system, as he attempts somewhat inefficiently to deal with too many stimuli at the same time.

It has also been found that activity level is a function of daily and monthly cycles, and is influenced by barometric pressure changes. Similarly with increased age, the activity level of normal children generally tends to lessen. Laufer and Denhoff, for example, found that hyperactivity of children with learning difficulties decreased from the twenty fifth to the thirty fifth year. Increased visual stimulation seems to increase activity, while the appearance of novel, odd and complex stimuli will often serve to reduce activity and focus attention.[11,6]

But despite theoretical arguments concerning causation and conflicting research findings concerning the effects of various remediation procedures upon hyperactivity, there is general agreement upon the axiom that a lack of control of motor functions accompanies and causes learning problems.

Thus, procedures which hold promise for reducing the purposeless activity of the distractible child are eagerly sought by teachers in special education. The following ones have been employed in various research studies,[8] in clinical settings,[4] as well as in classrooms within the Los Angeles City Schools during the past several years. They are not presented as the final answers, but as promising beginnings to the search for activities which may place the hyperactive child under better control. Further research should certainly validate the worth of these approaches, if indeed they are found to be valid. At the same time a search for refined methodologies should continue to take place.

RELAXATION TRAINING

In 1938 a book titled *Progressive Relaxation* outlined procedures which have to a large degree undergirded programs carried out during the intervening years by many psychiatrists, doctors of physical medicine and physical therapists.[3] The methods are intended to aid individuals relax by making them aware of residual muscular tensions over and above those needed to carry out life's activities. The procedures are designed to aid individuals gain self-control of their muscles, and some of the emotional factors contributing to excess tension. While it is true that muscular tension does not always reflect psychic upset; emotional disturbances, particularly in individuals who may habitually tense their muscles under stress, are likely to be reflected in excess, overt muscular activity of a chronic nature. In case studies of severely disturbed children and adults related in a recent symposium dealing with relaxation, it was reported that marked and significant changes occurred after such individuals were exposed to the relaxation techniques espoused by Jacobson. At times these techniques were accompanied by traditional psychotherapy, and, at other times, relaxation training was applied as the sole remedial technique. It was reported in this same publication that relaxation training is particularly appropriate for children, and that indeed they are often more receptive to this type of neuromotor education than are adults.[4]

In summary the techniques are as follows:

1. The individual or group members of a group are placed in as comfortable a position as possible with distracting stimuli removed. A teacher may, for example, ask the children to put their heads on their desks, and let their arms relax down in a vertical position. The children may be placed on their backs on mats, with a small roll under the knees so that the large leg muscles are relaxed due to the slightly bent position assumed by the legs.

2. Next the children should be talked into alternately tensing and then relaxing their total bodies and/or parts of their bodies using whatever verbal imagery

is appropriate to their intellectual and maturational level. Such directions as "make your muscles as hard as you can" . . . "tighten your stomach" . . . "hard . . . harder . . . " . . . "clench your fists as tightly as you can" and the like should be used.

3. Efforts should be made to do two primary things: (*a*) to help the child become aware of *degrees* of tension they can exert by saying "now tighten your muscles one-half that hard" or "now tighten your muscles one-fourth that hard" as he exerts maximum tension for from five to eight seconds followed by an intervening relaxation period; (*b*) to aid children become aware of unwanted tensions in *various parts* of the body, and indeed to become acutely aware of muscles and of muscle groups of which they may have become previously unaware. It is helpful, for example, to alternately tense and to relax various muscle groups, while moving from the head to the feet, and then up the body again . . . by saying "Tighten your jaw . . . harder . . . harder . . . now relax . . . now touch your shoulders . . . now make *them* tight . . . now relax . . . completely . . . make muscles in your arm . . . tighter . . . now make them as light as you can . . . take all the muscles out of your arm . . . etc.

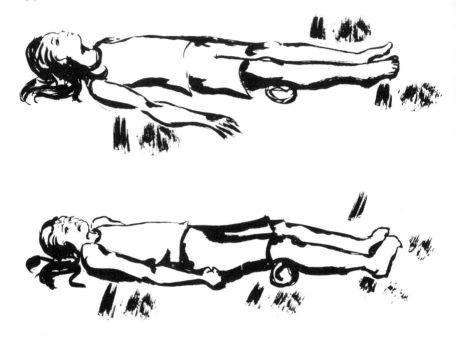

4. Movement of the purportedly relaxed limbs may be carried out to see if indeed some of the unwanted muscular tensions have dissipated. The child may be asked to lift his arm over his head, if standing or lying down, and then may be asked to let his arm fall of its own weight to his side, or to the mat if he is in a back lying position.

5. Special emphasis should be placed upon the muscles in the face, forehead, neck and jaw, for it is in these locations that general anxiety accompanied by muscular tension is most often reflected. Neck relaxation exercises are helpful if followed by slow head movements of a rolling nature to test just how much tension has been removed.

6. Various kinds of verbal imagery, of course, must be applied to children with various levels of intellectual ability. Directions to "tighten your sternoclediomastoid" will not be as effective as "make your neck loose" or "take the bones out of your muscles" when dealing with younger children. "Make yourself light . . . and then heavy . . . sink as far as you can into the mat" and similar general and simple directions are appropriate.

7. An effort should be made to help the child focus tension in specific body parts, while relaxing others. For example, he should be encouraged to tighten one arm only, and then the teacher or another child may test to see whether the other arm, and legs have remained relatively relaxed.

8. The teacher or another child may then check to see the extent to which a child has been able to direct tension into specific limbs and combinations of limbs when asked to do so. He may be asked to lift one arm, keeping his other arm and legs relaxed. The child may then be asked to move just his arm; later

to move an arm and leg on the same side, while keeping the limbs on the opposite side immobile and/or relaxed. The most difficult task, of course, is to move a limb and leg on opposite sides of the body (left arm and right leg) while keeping the two other body parts immobile. The teacher may make this kind of practice more difficult by asking the children to keep their eyes closed. Additionally, she may have to hold the limbs that she desires to remain immobile and/or at the same time aid the moving of the limbs by holding them and "starting them" herself.

Thus, relaxation training can be of a general nature and/or emphasize the ability to direct tension in specific parts of the body, attempting to eliminate the neuromotor "spillover" often seen in children with coordination difficulties. Relaxation of this nature should be given after children have been subjected to arousal producing activities (games, vigorous exercises, etc.) and prior to the time it is desired that they "calm down" and participate in various classroom tasks, or manual skills. Such training may also begin a program of perceptual-motor training, to be followed by other types of activities which are described in the paragraphs which follow.

Children with whom this type of training has been carried out have become so proficient that, if they become "too excited to work" . . . or "upset", they go into a corner, lie down and give *themselves* this training, at anytime during the school day. If as a group the children feel themselves becoming tense and upset, the whole class may engage in this kind of training led by the teacher. It is interesting to observe classes becoming aware of an excess of tension, which of course is socially transmitted, *requesting* relaxation training of their teacher, and then

returning to productive work following such training. It is interesting to note also that such hyperactive behavior is apparently not satisfying to these children. They do not like to be upset and they eagerly accept techniques offered to them for reducing their tensions.

In the program administered at University of California, Los Angeles, for some hyperactive children this kind of training constitutes about one-half of their total "lesson". For example, some engage in agility, balance, and ball handling activities for about one-half an hour, while during the final one-half hour they lie down in a dark indoor handball court, and learn how to relax, using the techniques outlined above.

PROLONGING ACTIVITIES

Another type of activity found helpful for aiding a child to gain control of himself is to present motor tasks which may be engaged in for progressively longer periods of time. The basic assumption underlying this component of the program is that, if a teacher can encourage a hyperactive child to perform a task longer than he has done anything before, his attention span may be prolonged in other tasks as well. Gross and fine motor activities are appropriate tasks for two reasons: (*a*) they seem to marshall several kinds of sensory stimulation at the same time (*i.e.,* visual, kinesthetic, etc.), and (*b*) prolonged attention or inattention to a motor task is easier to observe than is attention to tasks involving visual attention only.

A boy in our program we recently worked with came to us with an attention span of from five to eight seconds. After a few months' work with a single instructor, he was willing and able to engage in a variety of motor tasks for periods of time ranging from three to five minutes. These tasks consisted of walking lines of increasing length, drawing lines through patterns of increasing complexity on a blackboard, and attempting to keep a tennis ball balanced on a board 2 x 2 feet while holding the edges of the board in both hands.

The primary principle to keep in mind when attempting to "rivet" a distractible child's attention on tasks of this nature is that their complexity must be constantly changed, for, after some practice in the task, he may become able to perform it while giving relatively little of his visual attention to it. For example, if a balance beam is gradually lengthened (by adding additional beams to the end of the first one) as the child's skill improves, he may be found to be watching everything around the room while walking the beam. Thus it would be necessary in this case to place ropes at intervals across the beams so that he has to "watch his step" and keep his eyes upon the task at hand.

We once placed a hyperactive boy on a large wooden rocker and asked him to walk back and forth for increasing periods of time. At first the task was a challenge, and he walked gingerly, but willingly on the unsteady platform. Soon, however, we noted that his visual attention was drawn to everything around the room, while at the same time meeting the demands of the motor task. Therefore, to again readjust his attention upon the task at hand, we had to paint footprints on the level side of the rocker into which he was required to place his feet.

It becomes apparent, then, that a child can seem to attend to a task while performing it, but his visual attention, if the task is too easy or if it has been learned too well, may wander to innumerable other components of the environment. Therefore, initial attention to the task may be achieved by offering immediate rewards, knowledge of results (time he has accomplished the task), or some kind of reinforcement schedule. However, continued attention to the task will be maintained only if it is made increasingly challenging and difficult for the child.

It has been found that when rewards for execution of a task for prolonged periods of time are given, and/or when strict teacher supervision verbally "pressures" a child to do something for longer periods of time accompanied by immediate knowledge via a stopwatch, or the length of each attempt, many hyperactive children seem to be quite surprised to learn that they can slow themselves down. This knowledge and self-observation of performance becomes reinforcing in themselves. Many children with whom we have worked seemed to have discovered for the first time that they can slow down and place themselves under better control. They are pleased by the discovery, and begin to move at decreasing rates after gaining this information about themselves.

IMPULSE CONTROL

Closely associated with activities described in the preceding sections are tasks in which it is attempted to see just how slowly a child can move. Taken from the research by Maccoby[8] and others reviewed in Chapter 2 tasks should consist of those in which the total body is in motion as well as those in which the upper limbs are used while the body's center of mass remains fixed.

A child may be asked, for example, to see how slowly he can draw a line across the blackboard or how slowly he can walk a line. Competition may be utilized effectively with some groups of children such as having three children, starting from back-lying positions on a mat, see who can "get up last." The child up first is the loser!

In the case of some extremely hyperactive children, it may be necessary and helpful to reinforce them initially for periods of *immobility* prior to beginning this kind of impulse control training. Operant conditioning methods may be utilized effectively as a child is placed in a comfortable position and rewarded for periods of complete inactivity of increasing length. To some children, restrained movements may be tension producing, and relaxation training may be interpolated between such tasks. At the same time, if a hyperactive child or children begin to demonstrate that they can indeed move extremely slow, the teacher may attempt to see if they can be "turned on" ("How fast can you get up?") and then determine if they can place themselves under good control again ("How slowly can you do it now?").

Line drawing is a good activity to encourage slow controlled movement. Children may start from opposite sides of the blackboard, running their chalk down a narrow "road" composed of parallel lines. The child who gets across the board to meet her partner first is the loser!

Impulse control activities of this nature are often effective when accompanied

by music to give children an awareness in another sensory modality of just what slowness means. Indeed, all of the activities described in this chapter are many times more effectively carried out if appropriate music accompanies their application.

GENERAL CONSIDERATIONS

The reader is encouraged to grasp basic principles underlying the types of activities outlined on these pages. When and to whom the training should be applied is best determined by the constantly observing teacher, and cannot be exactly outlined by us. Learning is impeded by hyperactivity. Activities of this nature should not be placed on some kind of schedule, but should be given when they are needed by specific children. The weather, experiences prior to coming to school, the events of the school day, and similar variables radically change the levels of arousal of normal and atypical children on a daily and hourly basis. The sensitive teacher should thus insert activities to counteract these disrupting influences at *any time* that they are needed instead of waiting for the precise time that it is written on her schedule that some kind of perceptual-motor training should be carried out!

It should not be felt that all children in a given class need this kind of activity, though it is usual to find within populations of children with movement problems those who have to be "turned-on" as well as those who have to be "turned-down" or "off." Therefore, to encourage all members of a class (including the lethargic ones) to relax would not be sensible.

SUMMARY

Research has demonstrated that lack of attention and hyperactivity is disruptive to effective learning. Furthermore, there is evidence that specific training in self-control aids retarded and hyperactive children to be more productive in classrooms.

Three types of techniques are recommended to aid children place themselves under better control: (*a*) relaxation training in which the goal is to aid children to identify and to deal with disruptive residual muscular tensions, (*b*) prolonging motor tasks in which the effort is made to aid hyperactive children engage in motor tasks longer than they have engaged in anything before, and (*c*) impulse control activities in which it is attempted to demonstrate to children that they can slow themselves down and place themselves under better control by learning how slowly they may move in various ways.

It was recommended that these activities be applied wherever and whenever they appear needed by a given child or by a group of children within a classroom. Further research should refine and reject or expand some of the methodologies outlined on the preceding pages.

REFERENCES

1. Cromwell, Rue L., Baumeister, Alfred and Hawkins, William F.: "Research in Activity Level" (Chapter 20, 632–663), In Handbook of Mental Deficiency, Normal R. Ellis (Ed.), New York, McGraw-Hill Book Co., 1963.
2. Harrison, Wade, Lecrone, Harold, Temerlin, M. K. and Trousdale, W.: "The Effect of Music and Exercise Upon the Self Help Skills of Non-Verbal Retardates," *Am. J. Ment. Defic.*; *71*, 2, 279–282, 1966.

3. Jacobson, Edmund: *Progressive Relaxation,* Chicago, The University of Chicago Press, 1938.

4. ———: *Anxiety and Tension Control: A Physiologic Approach,* Philadelphia, J. B. Lippincott Co., 1965.

5. Kagan, Jerome: "Body Build and Conceptual Impulsivity in Children," *J. Person.; 34,* 118–128, 1966.

6. Laufer, M. W., Denhoff, E. and Solomons, G.: "Hyperkinetic Impulse Disorder in Children's Behavior Problems," *Psychosom. Med.; 19,* 38–49, 1957.

7. McKinney, J. P.: *A Multidimensional Study of the Behavior of Severely Retarded Boys,* Doctoral Dissertation, Ohio State University, 1961, (Unpublished).

8. Maccoby, Eleanor E., Dowley, Edith M., and Hagen, John W.: "Activity Level and Intellectual Functioning in Normal Pre-School Children," *Child Devel.; 36,* 761–769, 1965.

9. Ounsted, C.: "Hyperkinetic Syndrome in Epileptic Children," *Lancet; 2,* 303–311, 1955.

10. Semmel, M. I.: "Arousal Theory and Vigilance Behavior of Educable Mentally Retarded and Average Children," *Am. J. Ment. Defic.; 70,* 38–47, 1965.

11. Zeaman, David and House, Betty J.: "The Role of Attention In Retardate Discrimination Learning" (Chapter 5, 159–223), *Handbook of Mental Deficiency,* Norman R. Ellis (Ed.), New York, McGraw-Hill Book Co., 1963.

12. Zeaman, D., House, Betty J., and Orlando, R.: "Use of Special Training Conditions in Visual Discrimination Learning With Imbeciles," *Am. J. Ment. Defic.; 63,* 453–459, 1958.

6

Scribbling, Drawing and Writing

During the first days of birth, the infant evidences an awareness of movement in space and shortly after that time looks at his own moving hand.[9] It is not until many months later, however, that he gains the ability to hold a writing implement and to demonstrate graphically his awareness of some of the dimensions of space and form. From the time he first looks at objects in space to the time the child acquires writing skill lie several general and many specific sub-skills. Before he can scribble, for example, the child must be able to hold a writing implement with a reasonable degree of facility. Some of the sub-stages in the development of drawing ability might include:

1. Looks at writing implements, may hold them, and watches others make marks with them.
2. Crude scribbling seemingly at random, without producing any coherent design;
3. Rudimentary space perception evidenced by coloring within the general outlines of a figure;
4. Ability to stay within a design, and accurate drawing of figures;
5. The reproduction of more complex designs, and drawing pictures of objects.
6. Prints numbers and letters;
7. Acquires handwriting skills, with decreasing amounts of visual monitoring of movements needed, *i.e.,* can write without the need for constantly watching his moving hand.

Kellogg[5] identified five similar steps in the acquisition of hand-control when drawing and writing, including: the scribbling stage, drawing diagrams, combinations of diagrams (combined stage), more complex designs incorporating three or more diagrams (aggregate stage), and the final stage in which pictures are made with varying degrees of accuracy (pictorial stage).

Within each one of these general areas, however, innumerable sub-tasks have been identified by various authors. Kellogg, for example, has identified approximately 20 steps within the "scribbling" stage.

Obtaining exact developmental norms for graphic skills of children are difficult because innumerable variables can modify the accuracy of a child's attempts to scribble, draw, and write. For example, whether a child may choose to use a writing implement at all is dependent upon how much of this activity he observes within his home. Culturally deprived children may thus be at a disadvantage in this respect, since their parents, in their struggle for a living, may not have the time to join them in mutual endeavors involving coloring and drawing.

Other environmental supports will also influence the accuracy of a child's drawings. Imitation of another's drawing movements will sometimes produce more accurate attempts than will spontaneous attempts on the part of the child without the presence and/or stimulation of another person.

At the same time the child's accidental movements, as he makes various kinds of marks on a page, may prove self-reinforcing and lead to the pursuance of drawing and refining forms. For example, an accidental spiral or circular movement of the arm, producing a corresponding circle or spiral or series of spirals on a page, will be usually enjoyed by the child. He may then attempt consciously to reproduce the pattern which originally resulted from a chance movement.

Ample educational materials are available which purport to stimulate drawing abilities in children. Essentially two basic principles will aid in selecting the type of material best suited to stimulate a child to draw. One type of activity should permit the child to use his arms, wrists, and hands in free and relaxed movement patterns (have children draw circles on the blackboard using one hand and then using both hands simultaneously). The other idea is to develop the ability of a child to reproduce patterns with some degree of accuracy by tracing around various forms of objects.

Other controversies underlie the development of drawing and writing abilities in children. The majority of educators advocate that a child should be encouraged to draw with increasing accuracy within the lines of coloring books and similar tasks, while art educators maintain that too early restriction of a child's attempts to draw will inhibit his creative potential.

On the pages which follow, several facets of children's drawing behaviors are examined in detail. Initially, the developmental sequences lying within some of the more general areas of maturation presented previously are outlined. Next various remedial techniques are listed and evaluated. The concluding sections of the chapter contain the normative data gathered from a study of form drawing which we recently completed together with findings outlining the change which was elicited from children with drawing difficulties after their participation in a perceptual-motor training program.

DEVELOPMENTAL SEQUENCES

The Scribbling Phase.   Between the fifteenth and eighteenth months of life, as the child begins to exploit objects in various ways (*i.e.,* throwing, hitting, stacking), he may also begin to imitate scribbling movements by watching another child or adult. Such movements usually begin as simple tentative marks. However, as the child gains more confidence, these scribbling movements become bolder, more repetitive, complex and refined.

His first drawings are shaky lines, horizontal, vertical, or radiating from a central spot.* Within a few weeks, if writing implements continue to be made available, he will begin to draw patterns in which vertical and/or horizontal lines are repeated. This early developmental phase is indicated below:

Initial lines, dots.

Repetitive vertical, radial, and horizontal lines.

By about the eighteenth month, the child may begin to react to forms as he scribbles. Behavior such as that which follows will often be seen:

1. He will tend to "block-out" a form placed on a page, if it is a small one.
2. If the form is large enough (about 6 x 6 inches), the child may begin to scribble reasonably well within its confines.

*Neither information from available research studies, nor the results of clinical observations of children give conclusive evidence concerning whether the tendency to make horizontal, vertical, or lateral lines appears first. It seems that as children *scribble,* the three configurations are likely to appear with about equal probability. However, as children are asked to *draw figures with accuracy,* lateral lines are apparently more difficult.

3. The child may also attempt to balance his scribbling movements on a page by marking on the side of a sheet of paper that is opposite an already present figure. The following illustrates this phenomenon:

Shortly thereafter, usually about the twenty-fourth month, semicircular lines and initial attempts to enclose space will appear. First attempts will be irregular, but later attempts will consist of repetitive loops and spirals. This second phase includes:

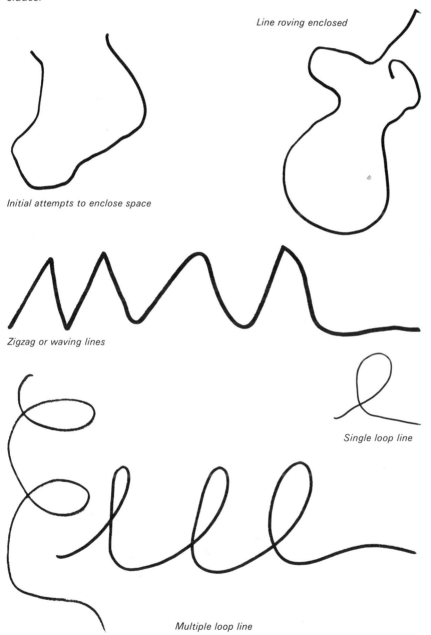

Line roving enclosed

Initial attempts to enclose space

Zigzag or waving lines

Single loop line

Multiple loop line

During these initial attempts, the child may begin to evidence hand preference, though the hand used will vary from time to time. It is helpful if the parent will observe any preference which emerges during these early attempts at graphic representation. Eberhard [1] has contributed research which indicates that manipulative movements are a product of central thought processes as well as of hand musculature. The "eye-thinking" practice, then, that a child obtains during these early scribbling attempts are as important as the practice obtained by the specific hand employed.

The next phase in the scribbling sequence involves drawing various spiral-shaped movements with the child's hand remaining stationary. If he uses his left hand to draw these spiral shaped movements, usually they are done in a clockwise direction and if he uses his right hand, they are usually done in a counterclockwise direction. Steps within this sequence are:

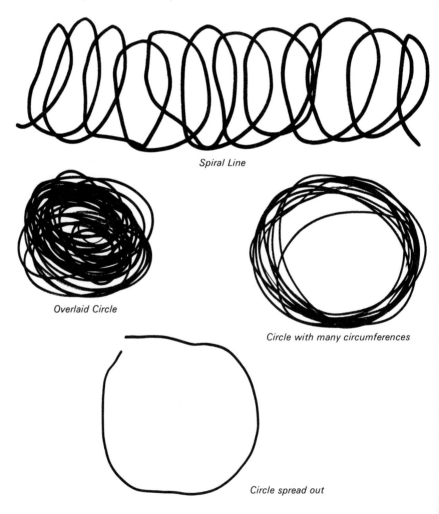

Spiral Line

Overlaid Circle

Circle with many circumferences

Circle spread out

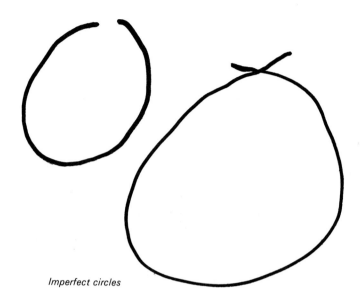

Imperfect circles

The Diagram Phase. The "diagram" phase which occurs next overlaps the "scribbling" stage in time. For example, it is not unusual to find that a child may, during the scribbling stage, accidentally, and later imitatively, form a cross by intersecting two lines, vertical and horizontal. Interesting studies of primate drawing behavior indicate that primates can also reproduce such a primitive diagram.[7] In humans, the first crosses appear as multiple scribbles crossing other multiple scribbles. Here are examples of these early crossing configurations:

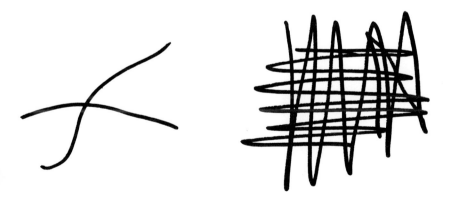

By the age of three, a child can usually reproduce a circle copied from a card. The degree of accuracy with which the child accomplishes this feat is presented in the concluding portion of this chapter.

With the passing of time, squares are produced. Three conditions affect the appearance of the first squares in children's drawings: (*a*) multiple crosses accidentally assume a squarelike pattern; (*b*) circles gradually begin to square off; and/or (*c*) the sides of the paper on which the child is writing is being reacted to. As the child nears the age of four, he can usually copy a square with reasonable accuracy. Steps involved in the ability to copy a square are enumerated below:

(a) Accidental square-making, arising from vertical and horizontal line drawing and cross-making.

(b) Squaring off circles.

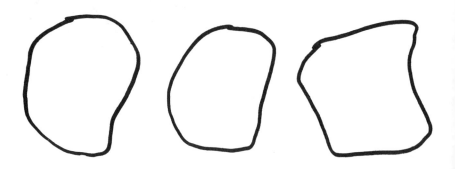

(c) Reaction to the sides of the paper.

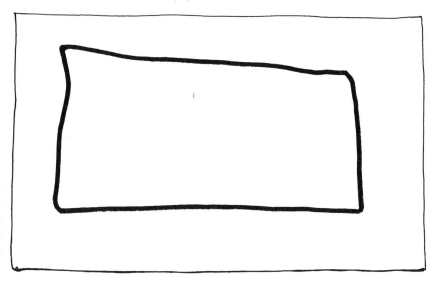

The first squares drawn are produced by lifting the hand after each side; only at about the age of five can a child reproduce a square with one continuous movement. As the ability to draw squares well is developed, the child becomes proficient in drawing accurate circles.

Although there are conflicting reports in the literature, it appears that the ability to draw figures arises from modifications of scribbling behavior rather than as reactions to external stimuli. Following this stage, the child will begin to draw irregular figures by combining curved and straight lines; he will usually become able to draw triangles and diamonds by seven.

First attempts to incorporate lateral lines into form drawing will usually be accompanied by rotating the paper. In essence, then, the child will still be drawing vertical and horizontal lines in constructing these figures. Later the child will be able to maintain a constant and straight orientation to the paper, keeping the paper parallel with the edge of the desk as he reproduces triangles and diamonds. Crosses incorporating lateral lines will also be used during these latter phases.

A recent study completed at our laboratory (and not published as yet) has produced findings which contribute to our understanding of the accuracy with which children of various ages draw basic geometric forms. One hundred seventy-nine children ranging in age from four to eight years were tested individually. While inspecting a circle, square, rectangle, triangle and diamond, the children were asked to draw an accurate copy of each figure.*

The four year olds could draw squares fairly accurately, but fifty per cent could not seem to close their circles. The four year olds were unable to draw rectangles, triangles or diamonds with any degree of accuracy.

*A detailed explanation of the scoring and administration of this test is found in the Appendix, p. 196.

By the age of five, the children were able to draw fair circles (closing them most of the time), squares, and rectangles, but still could not draw triangles or diamonds well.

The six year olds show a significant increase in their ability, when compared to the five year olds, to draw triangles and diamonds; and drew squares and circles equally as well as the five year olds.

The seven year olds were significantly better than the six year olds in the ability to draw squares, rectangles, triangles, and diamonds. The abilities of the eight year olds and the seven year olds did not differ significantly, thus suggesting that figure drawing ability in children tends to plateau about the age of seven.

Typical of the efforts of the children of various ages are the following:

	Circle	Square	Rectangle	Triangle	Diamond
Four Years					
Five Years					
Six Years					
Seven Years					
Eight Years					

Several other interesting findings emerged upon inspection of the data. Consistent from age to age and from figure to figure was the tendency of the more difficult figures to be drawn smaller than the easier ones. A size score was attached to each figure, and compilation of these indicated that given a figure to copy of the same size, rectangles were drawn smaller than squares, while the more difficult diamond was drawn smaller than the easier triangle. This tendency to restrict the size of the more difficult figures was slightly more pronounced in the older children.

Contrary to a common supposition, it was found that most children had more difficulty drawing an accurate circle than when asked to reproduce a square. At the same time, many of the children seemed to resist the simplicity of the drawing assignment given to them, and invariably requested to draw faces in the circles, to make houses out of the triangles, and in other ways attempted to make the tasks more interesting. A detailed analysis of the *methods* used by the right-handed children in this investigation when drawing the various configurations produced the following findings.*

DRAWING CIRCLES. It was usual to find that a child began to draw a circle in the upper right hand portion, and usually proceeded clockwise at the age of five,

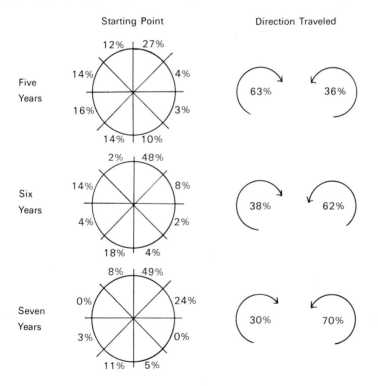

*The analysis is based upon the drawings of 46 five year olds, 50 six year olds, and 37 seven year olds, all right-handed children. The methods used by the left-handed children were not analyzed, as there were only 4, 7, and 5 subjects respectively in the three age groups.

with the tendency to draw counterclockwise more likely to be observed among the six and seven-year-old right-handers. The graphs below portray the percentage of children of each age group beginning at various portions of the circle, and the percentage of children traveling in each direction.

DRAWING SQUARES, RECTANGLES, TRIANGLES, AND DIAMONDS. Three percentages were obtained upon tabulating the drawing methods of the children as they copied squares, rectangles, triangles, and diamonds; (a) the percentage starting at various portions in the figures, (b) the percentage who drew the figures continuously without lifting their pencils from the paper, and (c) the direction the children who drew continuously traveled with their pencils around the figures. The results are summarized below.

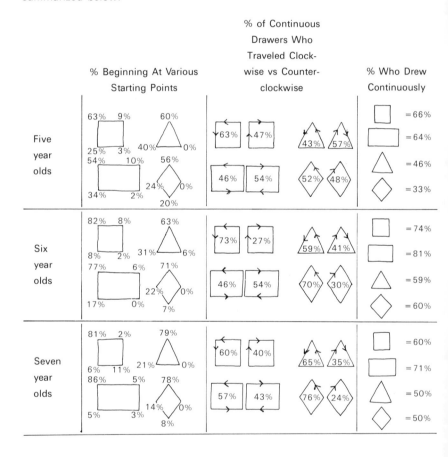

It is thus apparent upon inspection of these findings that, as might be expected, with increasing age children tend to draw these figures in a more continuous manner. In general, these right-handed children began their rectangles and squares in the upper left-hand corners. When drawing the more difficult triangles and diamonds, they began in the top corners and usually proceeded in a counterclockwise direction. Analysis of the directions the right-handed children of five years took when drawing all the figures reveals no clear-cut trends. They were as likely to move in a clockwise as in a counterclockwise direction. However, by the age of six and seven, most of the children drew the figures by moving their pencils in a counterclockwise direction.

AGGREGATES AND COMBINES. Two overlapping phases in drawing behavior occur next. (*a*) Two forms will be placed in simple combinations to form patterns, and (*b*) these in turn will be incorporated into complex patterns, using three or more simple forms. Combines are combinations of two forms, while aggregates may be defined as combinations of more than two separate forms. Examples follow.

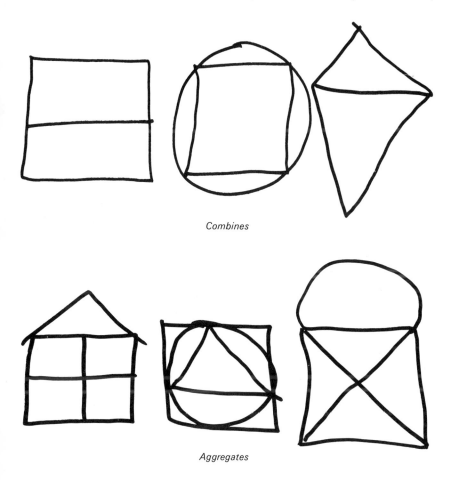

Combines

Aggregates

It has been hypothesized that the drawing of these latter types of figures by a child is influenced by teacher and parental stimulation. However, the intrinsic interest to the child for drawing such figures undoubtedly plays an important part in their practice.

A portion of the test developed for the assessment of graphic behavior of children measures the ability to reproduce an "aggregate" of a complex nature. Recently this test has been given to 179 children, ages four to eight years, and the following results have emerged.* The task involves drawing one-by-one figures added to the corners of a square which the child first draws after observing the examiner draw it. The child is given an opportunity to see each new figure added to the total configuration so that the final pattern appears like this (reduced in size).

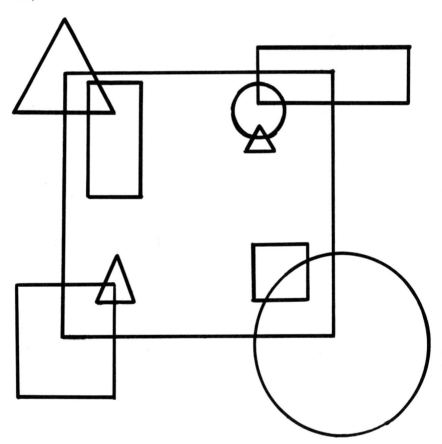

1. At the age of four, the children did not overlap any of the figures, preferring to draw them separately. In addition, as would be expected, most of the figures appear as rounded squares or as "squared-off" circles. The inability to reproduce triangles and rectangles was apparent. Most of the four year olds could not locate any of the figures in proper relationship to each other (or perhaps did not feel it was important!).

*Detailed test administration, scoring, and results are found in the Appendix, p. 196.

2. By five the children were able to overlap one or two figures, and to locate 4 or 5 out of the 10 figures correctly. The triangles began to appear differently than the squares and circles at this age.

3. By six years of age, the children became able to locate most of the figures accurately (usually about 7 or 8 out of 10), and could draw the various figures reasonably well.

Typical of the Drawings in This
Task at Various Ages

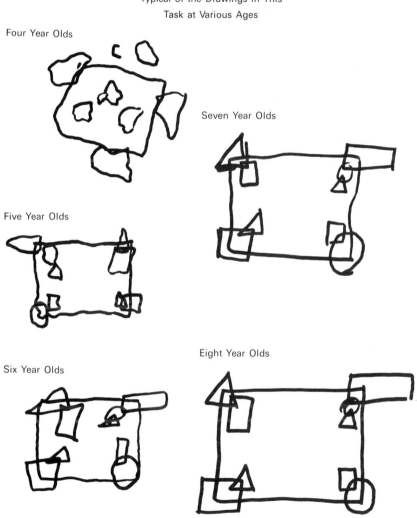

Four Year Olds

Five Year Olds

Six Year Olds

Seven Year Olds

Eight Year Olds

Pictorial Phase. The final stage in graphic behaviors has been termed the pictorial phase. Simple pictures which usually consist of familiar objects, houses, trees, the sun, and people are attempted by the child during this phase.

7

The several stages through which the child passes in his attempts to draw human figures are:

a. Circles with marks in them or around them.

b. Circles with marks in and around them.

c. Circles with approximate representations of the parts of the face.

d. Round faces with legs and arms coming directly from the face.

e. The appearance of fingers and trunk.

f. The increased refinement of the figure, including emphasis on eyes, eyebrows, fingers, feet and attempts at facial expression.

By the age of five and six, then, the child deliberately draws parts of his environment, instead of producing them accidentally. Pictorial representations of depth and perspective appear in their drawings at about the age of eight and nine, while further refinements, including shading, appear later. These more advanced skills are highly related to any special training the child might have received during middle and late childhood.

Cursive Writing Versus Block Printing. Between the seventh and eighth years, the child may be confronted with the problems of cursive writing, having earlier attempted to block print letters and numbers. A controversy exists concerning whether a child should first learn to print or to write cursively. Some arguments in favor of block printing are:

1. Block printing is not as difficult as cursive writing, nor does it require as much control.
2. If all cursive writing required the natural forward moving loops, it might be assumed to be the easier and more ''natural'' of the two, since it appears earlier in the infants life. However, the frequent back-tracking required when writing s's, q's and the like are not ''natural'' movements.

Arguments in favor of cursive writing include:

1. Cursive writing is more rhythmic than the disjointed block printing.
2. Letter reversal is not seen in cursive writing, while it is often found among five and six year olds attempting to print various asymmetrical letters and numbers.

After this very brief summary of the arguments favoring the two methods of teaching writing, a few general conclusions may help in determining which one to use. It would seem that some kind of modified block printing might be best for many children initially. It must be certain that movement patterns opposite to those later required for specific letters in cursive writing are not imposed on the child during this early block-printing training. Other children may profit from initial exposure to cursive writing, particularly those whose hand-eye control is reasonably well developed, and whose early attempts at spiral sequences seem relaxed and accurate.

Below are summarized sequences through which normal children usually pass in their attempts to acquire hand-eye control in drawing and writing movements.

REMEDIAL PROGRAMS

Two primary objectives are to be found in the various methods used to improve children's drawing and writing abilities. One aim is to achieve more relaxation in writing movements. The second goal is to increase the control of writing movements.

It is believed desirable to combine tasks in programs of remediation which employ activities designed to enhance both accuracy and fluid movement. The

CHART 23

Drawing and Writing Movements

AGE (In years-months)	BEHAVIOR
0.1–1	Accidental and imitative scribbling.
1–1.6	Refinement of scribbles, vertical and horizontal lines, multiple line drawing, scribbling over visual stimuli.
2–3	Multiple loop drawing, spiral, crude circles. Simple diagrams evolve from scribblings by the end of the second year.
3	Figure reproduction to visually presented figures, circles, and crosses.
4	Laboriously reproduces squares, may attempt triangles but with little success.
4.6–5	Forms appear in combinations of two or more. Crude pictures appear (house, human form, sun). Can draw fair squares, crude rectangles, and good circles, but has difficulty with triangles and diamonds.
6–7	Ability to draw geometric figures matures. By seven can draw good circles, squares, rectangles, triangles, and fair diamonds.

teacher should alternate between the two types of tasks; if a child appears to be able to make relaxed coordinated movements in relatively large amounts of space, he should then require smaller more accurate movements. If attempting to make accurate movements required in block printing of letters and numbers appears to manifest itself in a tense, restricted manner, the educator should insert arm-freeing movement tasks into the program.

The overriding objective of programs designed to remediate hand-eye coordination in drawing tasks should be the development of a child who is flexible (*i.e.,* one who can write on a variety of writing surfaces in a number of planes, and one who can execute a number of types of movements in all directions relative to his body). The educator, then, should develop a program in which the child's nervous system is afforded a large variety of neuromotor "programs" so that his drawing-writing behavior will meet all academic and artistic contingencies with which he will be confronted.

Types of arm-hand-freeing exercises.

1. Repetitive circles, loops which "travel" . . .

2. Repetitive circles, figure 8's, in all planes which remain relatively fixed . . .

3. Repetitive lines in various planes, using large amounts of space . . . copied on blackboards, and/or on large sheets of paper . . .

We have not encountered any evidence that two-handed drawing tasks in which both arms move simultaneously, advocated by some authorities,[2] are productive of more efficient one-handed drawing accuracy. It would seem that practice time should be devoted primarily to one-handed movements with the child's preferred hand when executing the above exercises.

Hand preference may be assessed by noting the tendency of a child to use one hand or the other in 5 or 6 difficult (for him) one-handed tasks done during several testing periods, repeated at regular intervals for one or two weeks. His preferred hand should be considered the hand most used in these tasks, even though the tendency to do so may be slight.

4. Drawing in many directions in several planes.

5. Drawing kinesthetically.

Types of accuracy-producing exercises.

1. Channel drawings

2. Dot-connecting

3. Template tracing

One of the more helpful methods of encouraging accurate hand-eye coordinations that are needed in drawing and writing has been outlined by Kephart, Strauss, and others.

1. Initially, it is suggested that the hand be guided through various line and figure drawing tasks by the teacher. The child's hand should be held, and he should be encouraged to watch its movements as it is pulled through a number of desired configurations.

2. If the child does not require manual guidance, he may be confronted with apparatus which permit him to move a pencil or some other writing instrument in grooves shaped as circles, squares, and the like.

3. When the child is able to perform the exercises in #2 above (*i.e.* he does not "jam" the pencil in the groove, nor does he retrace his progress), he may be asked to draw various figures within shallow pans of modeling clay (about ¼ inch deep). This exercise, while more difficult than drawing in channels, involves a media which to some degree "grabs" the writing instrument and prevents small inaccuracies in movement from becoming magnified.

4. After competency in drawing accurate figures in clay is acquired the teacher should present various patterns over which the child can trace. Various geometric figures, as well as line drawing of various shapes and in several directions, may be included in this portion of the training program.

5. The final step requires that the child draw various patterns without tracing. Patterns are presented visually for the child to inspect and to copy. Then, the patterns should be visually presented for shorter periods of time before the child is permitted to start drawing, thereby enhancing his visual memory. A final stage would involve offering verbal directions concerning the type of line and/or geometric figure the teacher expects the child to draw.

In a recently completed study in our laboratory, the composite form drawings of 65 children were scored before and after participating in a program of motor education encompassing *primarily big muscle activities,* agility, balance, and the like. The mean time between the pre- and post-test was five months, and three scores were obtained reflecting whether the child copied the figures' sizes accurately, the accuracy with which they drew the figures, and whether they located the figures correctly as they added them to the diagram. Analysis of the findings revealed that while no significant difference was obtained in the accuracy or size of the drawings when contrasting pre- and post-test scores, highly significant changes were obtained in the accuracy with which they *located* the figures on the various corners of the original square they drew to start the exercise. Out of a possible 10 points for locating each of the 10 figures correctly, the group of 65 with an average age of 8.92 (SD = 2.48), containing 58 boys and 7 girls, scored 5.29 (SD = 3.47) prior to participating in the program while the final score achieved on this type of complex drawing form drawing test was 7.04 (SD = 3.35), a difference significant at the 1 per cent level of confidence (t = 5.68).* It thus appeared that participation in activities involving total body movement may have contributed to the ability to organize figures in space when drawing on a page, although further research is needed before such a claim may be substantiated. A control group containing similar children is presently being tested in order to further validate this finding.

SUMMARY

A survey of the literature reveals several overlapping stages in the development of scribbling and drawing in children. By the age of five years, children begin to draw reasonably accurate squares and circles, but are unable to draw triangles and diamonds. By the age of seven, the ability to draw geometric figures and to locate them relative to each other tends to mature.

As a child matures, he tends to, if right-handed, draw geometric figures in a continuous manner in a counterclockwise direction. The more difficult figures are drawn smaller than simpler ones, other things being equal.

Remedial techniques for drawing should include tasks intending to improve accuracy, as well as those which encourage freedom of hand-arm movement. Accuracy may be improved by first guiding a child's hand, then asking him to draw through grooves; and if this can be accomplished, he may then draw in clay, later being asked to trace over figures, and finally, making free-hand figures of complexity. "Arm freeing" exercises should be engaged in, in various planes, and in various directions, relative to the child's body.

REFERENCES

1. Eberhard, Ulrich: "Transfer of Training Related to Finger Dexterity," *Percept. & Mot. Skills, 17,* 274, 1963.
2. Getman, G. N. and Kane, Elmer R.: *The Physiology of Readiness—An Action Program For the Development of Perception for Children,* Minneapolis, Minnesota, P.A.S.S. Inc., 1964.
3. Goodenough, F. L.: *Measurement of Intelligence by Drawings,* Yonkers, New York, World Book Co., 1926.
4. Illingworth, R. S.: *The Development of the Infant and Young Child—Normal and Abnormal,* 3rd Edition, Edinburgh, E. & S. Livingstone Ltd., 1967.

*The mean improvement which would be expected within a five-month interval according to normative data in our possession is .86 points; while the experimental group in this study evidenced a change of 1.75 points during this same time interval.

5. Kellogg, Rhoda: *What The Child Scribbles and Why,* Palo Alto, California, National Press, 1955.

6. Machover, Karen: *Personality Projection in the Drawing of the Human Figure (A Method Of Personality Investigation),* Springfield, Charles C Thomas, 1949.

7. Morris, Desmond: *The Biology of Art—A Study of the Picture-Making Behavior of the Great Apes and Its Relationship to Human Art,* New York, Alfred A. Knopf, 1962.

8. Swenson, C. H.: ''Empirical Evaluations of Human Figure Drawings,'' *Psychol. Bull.; 54,* 431–466, 1954.

9. White, Burton L. and Held, Richard: ''Plasticity of Sensorimotor Development in the Human Infant,'' *The Causes of Behavior: Readings In Child Development and Educational Psychology,* Judy F. Rosenblith and Wesley Allinsmith (ed.), Boston, Allyn Bacon, 1966.

7

Strength, Flexibility, and Endurance

It is common finding that children with skill problems are also unfit.[5] Fitness usually implies some kind of efficiency encompassing performance in tasks which require muscular strength, flexibility, and/or cardiovascular endurance. Children who are clumsy are frequently excluded from games by their more capable peers, and thus have less opportunity to participate vigorously.

It thus appears that, in the main, intervening variables may produce lack of muscular fitness in atypical children. Poor experiences in vigorous activities results in less inclination to perform which results in less performance efficiency due to deterioration of the muscular and cardiovascular apparatus. Improving the fitness of most children will not come simply by prescribing strict exercise regimens. A child, when asked to do 10 or 20 pushups, is many times not aware of the long-term ''good'' these exercises will do him; he is usually only concerned with the emotional content of his experiences; are the exercises fun or oppressive? If they are unpleasant, it is unlikely that he will ''overload'' himself and perform the exercises with vigor. Unless strength exercises or endurance activities place some strain on the child, it is not to be expected that real change will occur. Thus one of the primary problems when improving the general fitness of unfit children is to motivate them to participate vigorously. We believe that an increased tendency to participate in vigorous activities comes about when the child perceives he is becoming more competent in the skills required. Thus, skill improvement would seem to be a more productive way to improve general and specific measures of muscular and respiratory fitness than simply prescribing exercises.

Acting on this principle, only about five minutes at the end of an hour of physical activity is devoted specifically to fitness exercises in a program which we administer at the University of California at Los Angeles.* A comparison of scores elicited by 65 children (mean age = 8.92) (SD = 2.48) in a pre-post test scores

*It is surprising how physical educators working with children persist in administering vigorous exercises intended to overload the child's muscular systems at the *beginning* of the physical education period, instead of at the *end* of the period where such exercises more properly belong.

separated by five months of twice a week classes was made; the following findings emerged:

1. The scores in all fitness given evidenced statistically significant gains, exceeding the 1 per cent level of confidence. For example, pushup scores changed from a mean of 7.24 (SD = 4.11) to 9.33 (SD = 3.32) (t = 4.19).

2. Abdominal strength increased; pre-test sit-up (bent knees) mean score was 4.78 (SD = 3.59), while the group average at the completion of the testing period was 6.37 (SD = 3.51) (t = 4.04).

3. The children were able to pull better in a modified pull-up task in which the child from a back lying position attempted to pull himself, stiff-body, up to a bar held $2\frac{1}{2}$ feet off the ground, while keeping his heels on the ground. Pretest mean was 3.11 pulls (SD = 3.29), while after five months, the average score of the 65 children was 5.80 (SD = 3.90), (t = 4.86).

4. A measure of lower back strength was obtained by requiring the child to see if he could raise his shoulders, head and arms off the floor, while holding his heels, in a front-lying position, for twenty seconds. The score obtained was the time he could accomplish this with a maximum score of 20 (seconds) possible. Pre-test mean was 14.37 seconds (SD = 6.71) while a post test average was 17.00 (SD = 4.73) (t = 2.93).

(Seven girls and 58 boys were subjects in this study.)

During the first part of the hour, however, the children in this program performed a number of vigorous activities which undoubtedly contributed to the improvement shown. For example, ample time was usually allotted for trampoline jumping, an activity which requires rigid tension in the abdominal, stomach, and leg muscles as the child contacts the bed in order to achieve maximum height on successive bounces. Indeed, the child will receive an uncomfortable whiplash type of reaction if he is limp when he contacts the bed of the trampoline.[*]

A survey of the literature suggests that the following principles should be observed when exposing children to exercise regimes:

1. Passively performing exercises without any overload of the muscular and/or cardiovascular system will not result in any significant improvement of endurance or strength. Exercises must attempt to extend the child's limits; he must in some way be encouraged to work hard.

2. Strength exercises performed through a range of motion are probably superior to those in which static isometric pushing and pulling are engaged in, particulary when improvement in limb strength is desired. Static exercises for the improvement of trunk strength are sometimes desirable.

3. Endurance in muscular exercises can be improved if several are administered in rapid succession with little rest between each. A circuit exercise program is described on page 103.

4. Muscular flexibility may be improved most by requiring the muscle or muscle group to stretch for prolonged periods of time, rather than imposing the bouncing and stretching movements as has been the practice in the past.[4] The latter type of movement performed rapidly may impede the acquisition of flexibility

---

[*]Despite the pseudo-scientific theories advanced by some for improvement in children through trampolining, it is believed that the main benefits derived may be explained by improvement of trunk-leg fitness due to regular and vigorous demands made upon the anti-gravity muscles when bouncing.

by damaging the tendinous muscle sheath which may cause a group of muscles involved to further "tighten-up."

5. General strength and flexibility are incorrect concepts; rather, the exercise program should be designed to induce strength in various areas of the body through the applications of specific exercises.

6. Exercise regimens to lose weight without accompanying diet control are usually ineffective. Most children, and adults, can defeat most programs of vigorous physical exercises by overeating.

7. Fat in specific spots of the body cannot be "worn off" by exercising muscles underlying this fat. Children will gain and lose fat in specific areas of the body as they generally lose and gain body weight. The amount of fat coming off or being added to a specific body area is dependent upon the percentage of body fat characteristically carried by that individual in that area of his body.

STRENGTH

A complete catalogue of all possible strength exercises would encompass a manual many times the size of this one. The following exercises are intended to suggest types of activities and ways in which they might be employed. Books by Wallis and Logan[9] and others have outlined, in more detail, innumerable muscular fitness exercises for children than will be done here. Four primary areas of the body will be dealt with, and exercises projecting various degrees of intensity and difficulty are outlined on the following pages. Exercises for the shoulder-girdle, exercises for the abdominal region, exercises for the legs, and those intending to improve the strength of the lower back are contained on the following pages.

Arm-Shoulder Exercises. Pushing exercises aid the chest muscles, those in the front of the shoulder, and muscles which extend the arms. Examples of some appropriate ones for children include:

Wall Pushups.

8

These may be made more difficult by moving the child back further from the wall, and/or requiring the hands be placed further apart on the wall or closer than shoulder width.

Knee Pushups.

These also may be made more difficult when the hands are placed wider or narrower than shoulder width. When a child can do from 6 to 8, he should be encouraged to do:

Regular Pushups.

These are more difficult if the legs are raised about 1 foot as shown.

Pulling exercises are important for the upper back muscles. The "winged" scapulas frequently seen protruding from the backs of unfit children can be made to lie flat against the upper back if various pulling exercises are performed. For example:

Rope pulling, rising from a seat to a stand.

The child can "climb" and lower himself to a seated position again, using slow, controlled movements.

Horizontal pulling: hand-over-hand pulling can also be fun on a rope extending in horizontal directions; tug-of-war is a competitive pulling exercise.

If a child can perform the above exercises well, a modified pullup should be used. The feet should remain on the floor, and the body should remain straight as the pullup to a chest high bar is executed from 6 to 10 times.

Abdominal Lower Back.   Abdominal exercises while lying on the back are more effective if the knees are slightly bent, causing the large leg muscles to be excluded from the movement.

Simple abdominal "curls" become harder if the flexed position is held for from four to eight seconds.

Full situps are helpful, and if the child twists from side-to-side, more trunk muscles are involved.

Situps can be made easier if the child reaches forward with his hands; it is more difficult to keep the hands behind the head when doing them.

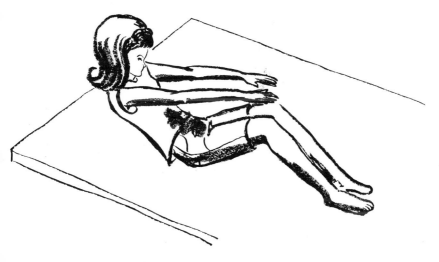

Lying on an incline, head down, of course, makes situps more difficult as does holding a weight behind the head. These latter two exercises are usually too difficult for most retarded children.

Simple back "extensions" are helpful when attempting to strengthen the lower back. If held from four to eight seconds, they become more effective. The ankles should be held down as shown, and the child should be encouraged to hold his arms in several different positions while performing them (i.e., behind his head, extended to the front, to the sides, etc.).

Back Extension.

Hands to the front in a back extension.

More difficult yet is when the child's upper body is permitted to drop below his hips while lying on a bench. Care must be taken to execute this modification slowly and should only be attempted when reasonable strength is evidenced in the simpler back extension movement described above.

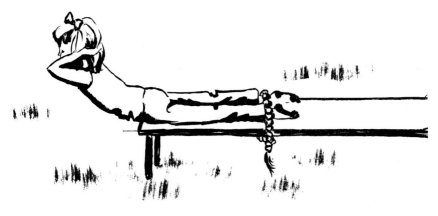

STRENGTH AND ENDURANCE

If strength exercises are performed within a short period of time, with little rest between each, cardiovascular endurance is enhanced. For example:

"Build-up pushups" (or any other exercise) can be accomplished by starting with one: jogging about 15 to 20 feet away and performing 2; jogging back to the original starting point and doing 3; and continuing until from 6 to 10 are performed at one of the "stations." A group of children can be exercised quickly in this way.

This type of exercise regimen may have two or three stations in which various kinds of exercises are performed at each, and in which the number of exercises are increased or decreased as each station is reached, for example:

This type of exercise program may aid in the control of children who are emotionally disturbed but physically competent. Care must be taken insofar as extreme fatigue can result from its use, due to the lack of recuperation time permitted between exercises. Higher motivation will result if exact daily records of improvement are kept for this, and for the other exercise programs outlined in these pages. This type of vigorous exercise will not usually "drain" the energies of hyperactive children. On the contrary, they may become more difficult to control as the intensity increases. Thus following such a vigorous regimen in such a program, when distractible children are being dealt with, a period should be permitted in which they may "calm down" using some of the activities outlined in Chapter 5.

ENDURANCE

Activities solely intended to improve cardiovascular endurance may also be engaged in productively. Such as:

Alternate jogging and walking.

A distance of about 300 yards should be used to start with, jogging 50 and walking 50 yards; this can be gradually increased as the children become able to accommodate to the various overloads.

Swimming and activities to train competitive swimmers are used by some educators with success on neurologically impaired children.

Kicking for distance on kickboards; keep track of improvement.

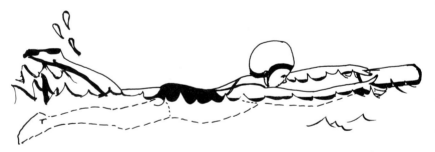

Swimming for distance; count laps from day to day.

Various running activities are helpful.

Distance in time; "How far can you go in five minutes?"

Time: "How long can you keep jogging?"

It is not to be expected that endurance gained by swimming will readily transfer to competency in running activities or vice-versa. Practice in this activity, since progress is easily measured and perceived by the participating children, however, may have desirable "side-effects", improvement of the self-concept.

MUSCULAR FLEXIBILITY

Stretching should be done slowly and using the limb or trunk to their full range of movement.

Slow reaching for the toes while seated or standing is helpful in achieving flexibility in the lower back and back-of-the-leg muscles.[4] If this is done too vigorously, particularly with fast-growing children in late childhood or early adolescence, minor or major damage to the heel tendon may result.

Arm stretching exercises are helpful, simple equipment (towels) may be used.

Child should not pull outward on towel, but should move arms back and forth to stretch at the shoulder.

Backward trunk flexibility as well as forward flexibility should be improved.

SUMMARY

Programs consisting solely of muscular exercises for children must be well motivated if they are to be beneficial. The duration of time devoted to them need not be prolonged, if the children are otherwise engaged in games and other developmental activities of a vigorous nature.

Records simple enough for the children to comprehend should be kept, so that progress may be observed by both participants and teachers. At times, several components of muscular and cardiovascular fitness may be improved at the same time as illustrated on page 103.

Fitness activities might be scheduled for from five to fifteen minutes, three times a week on a Monday-Wednesday-Friday basis, with the intervening days devoted to the improvement of manual dexterity and sports skills.

REFERENCES

1. AAHPER—Kennedy Foundation: Special Fitness Awards for the Mentally Retarded, Washington, D.C., NEA Publications.
2. Benda, Clemon, E.: *The Child With Mongolism,* New York, Grune & Stratton, 1960.
3. Cratty, Bryant J.: "Strength, Endurance Plus Flexibility Equals Fitness," Chapter VIII in *Developmental-Sequences of Perceptual-Motor Tasks,* Freeport, New York, Educational Activities, Inc., 1967.
4. DeVries, Herbert J.: Evaluation of Static Stretching Procedures for the Improvement of Flexibility, *Res. Quart.; 33,* 222–229, 1962.
5. Francis, R. J' and Rarick, G. L.: "Motor Characteristics of the Mentally Retarded," U.S. Office of Education Co-operative Research Project #152, University of Wisconsin, September, 1967.

6. Hayden, Frank J.: *Physical Fitness for the Mentally Retarded,* Washington, D.C., Joseph P. Kennedy Foundation, 1964.
7. Howe, Clifford: "A Comparison of Motor Skills of Mentally Retarded and Normal Children," *J. Except. Child.; 25*–8, 352–354, April, 1959.
8. Johnson, G., Orville: "A Study of the Social Position of Mentally Handicapped Children in the Regular Grades," *Am. J. Ment. Defic.; 55,* 60–89, 1950.
9. Wallis, E. and Logan G. A.: *Exercise for Children,* Englewood Cliffs, New Jersey, Prentice-Hall Inc., 1966.

8

Improvement of Large Muscle Control

It is difficult to separate motor acts into those in which only the larger muscles are used versus those in which small muscles are involved. For example, balancing incorporates extremely fine adjustments of larger as well as of smaller muscle groups; dribbling a basketball down the floor involves manipulative as well as big muscle skills, while the larger postural muscles stabilize his body as the child writes. Thus, if a child's seated balance is poor, it is likely he will experience problems in writing, while poor standing balance may influence negatively the ability to draw accurately on a blackboard.

The fine integration and timing of the various muscle groups of the body are imperative for the efficient performance of playground skills. The integration of the arms with the legs is important when jumping and throwing. Good coordination of one side of the body with the other is reflected in efficient running, walking, skipping, and in similar locomotor activities. Chapter 6 contained activities purporting to enhance motor control of the arm-eye action systems. This chapter contains types of activities to enhance balance, agility, and ball-handling skills.

BALANCE

Balance is rather basic to general motor performance. It is usually evaluated in tasks in which stress has been placed upon an individual as he attempts to orient his body to gravity in some way. Good balance depends upon the interaction of two primary systems; muscular feedback from postural muscles which control the ability to maintain an upright position, and the visual system which aids the individual to "tie-himself-down" to gravity when some kind of variable to cause disequilibrium has been imposed.

Several general considerations should be kept in mind when attempting to train a child to balance better.

1. Training should take place in several kinds of balance tasks including those in which some kind of visual stress is imposed (*i.e.,* eyes-closed balance tasks),

in tasks in which the child is asked *to move* and maintain his equilibrium (beam walking), as well as in activities in which his center of mass remains relatively fixed (static balances of various sorts).

2. Balancing may be made increasingly difficult for a child by imposing stress of several kinds.

a. The area on which the child is balancing may be made smaller (decrease with width of the balance beam).

b. Some kinds of visual stress may be imposed, ranging from the easiest (watch a stable point), through increasingly difficult, (no specific instructions about what should be looked at) to requiring the child to watch a moving point which moves from left to right across the line or beam the child is attempting to walk.

c. The platform on which the child is asked to balance may be made increasingly unstable. An example is asking him to balance on a small board with some kind of runner or knob underneath it.

d. In static balances the child's base of support may be decreased, or his center of mass may be raised *i.e.,* stand on one foot lift your arms (or knee) higher.

In data recently obtained in our laboratory, a .45 correlation was obtained when contrasting balance scores and scores from The Gates Reading Survey. Ismail has obtained similar low-moderate correlations between the same two measures.* It would thus appear that the visual-motor coordination underlying balance, to a slight degree, is predictive of reading success. A correlation of .4, however, only means that about 16 per cent of the manner in which children's reading scores arrange themselves (from the best to the worst) is predictable from knowing their balance scores. At the same time, there is no indication that improvement in balance scores will exert influence upon academic success. The improvement of balance because of its obvious causal relationships with other *motor* attributes is, however, important for its own sake. In a recent investigation completed in our laboratory, it was found that 71 per cent of 51 children, subjected to a program lasting four months in which balance training was a part, showed significant improvement of approximately one year on a maturational scale. It thus appears that improvement in balance may be elicited by the activities which follow:

1. *Static Balance.* Static balance tasks may involve posturing in standing positions of various kinds, and/or balancing in relatively stable positions on mats, with the arms, knees, elbows, head, etc., touching the mat. Generally, these activities should be made interesting to children by using various kinds of imagery. For example, it may be suggested that they make "bridges" with themselves over the "river" (lines drawn on the floor).

For example:

Low bridges, using various parts of the body in contact with the mat. Knees, hands, elbows, etc.

*Nineteen boys ages eight and nine years.

Higher bridges, using hands, feet, and combinations of each.

Bridges with the back toward the mat.

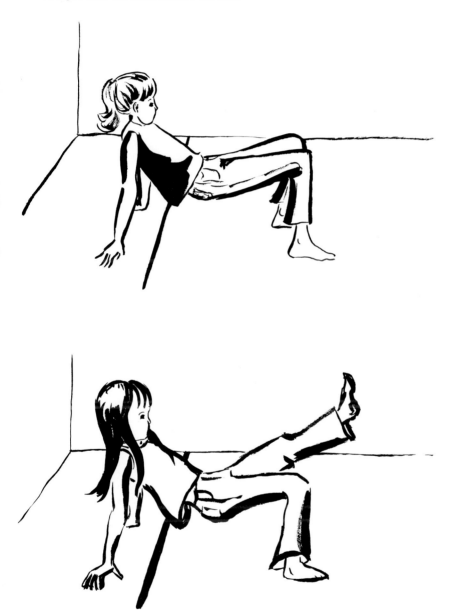

These games can, of course, be made into left-right training games, as the child is asked to remove certain arms and legs from the mat, or the balance on his left-foot and right-arm, etc. Later, the child can be asked to create various types of bridges, *i.e.,* use three parts of your body, one of which is an elbow; use two parts of your body, one of which is a knee.

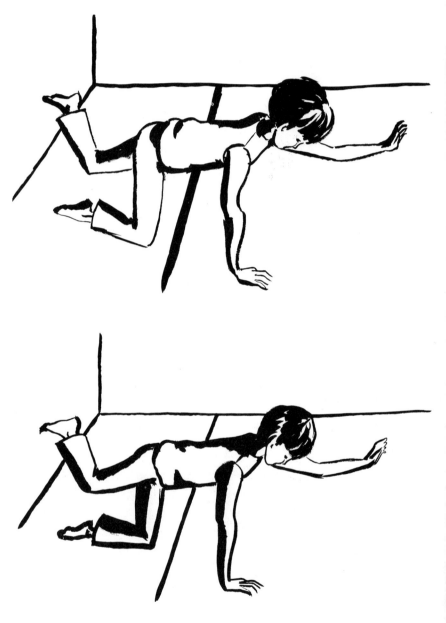

Various standing positions can be employed, with modifications of arms and leg positions which can be made increasingly difficult.

Line standing positions, both feet on lines in various ways . . . arms on shoulders, folded, and overhead . . . for added difficulty.

One foot stand positions, using preferred and non-preferred foot, with arms involved in the balance, folded in front of the body, on shoulders, over head.

Both "bridges" games and standing balances can be made easier if the child is asked to watch a point while balancing as shown.

At the same time, both types of static balancing activities can be made more difficult by asking the child to assume various of the positions with the eyes closed.

These same positions may be assumed on the trampoline for added difficulty.

Additional difficulty can be introduced if the standing positions are assumed, while asking the child to watch a moving point, *i.e.,* a ball swinging on a string.

Balance Platforms. The balance quality probably needed when skating, skateboarding, surfing and the like can be aided by using platforms that move on one or two axes as shown.

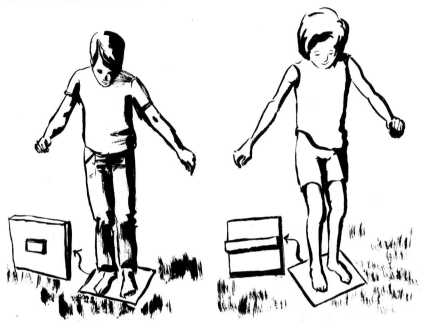

By modifying the positions the child stands, increasing difficulty can be introduced. Also, by either asking the child to fixate at a given point, or to close his eyes, or to watch moving points, *i.e.*, play catch with another child on a similar balancing platform, increased difficulty can be introduced.

Modifications of foot positions

Arm positions can be also modified

One-footed balances can be assumed

When a child is asked to assume the positions outlined in the previous illustrations, he should be given positions which he finds reasonably difficult to maintain, those which he can hold for from four to eight seconds. After he can maintain various positions for about eight to ten seconds, more difficult positions, visual stresses, balancing methods should be introduced.

MOVING BALANCES

You can vary the nature of the platform walked by raising it from lines on the floor to beams of various heights.

Narrow it . . .

Tilt it to the left or right . . .

Incline it for up-hill or down-hill walking . . .

Several children may be asked to perform various static balances at the same time using the width of the balance beam . . .

Other modifications of the surface may be made; objects may be placed on it to walk over . . .

Obstacles may be placed slightly above the surface of the beam . . .

Obstacles may be placed so that the child must walk under them . . .

You may ask the child to watch stable and later moving points as he becomes able to walk the beam with little effort.

Fixed points at the end of the beam . . . level with the eyes . . .

Fixed points to the side of the beam . . .

Moving points at the end of the beam moving up and down . . .

Moving points at the end of the beam, moving from side-to-side . . .

Moving points at the side of the beam, moving from side-to-side . . .

AGILITY MOVEMENTS

Agility movements of several kinds should be practiced by children, including those in which arm-leg integration is involved, those in which the body-movement is primarily up and down, and tasks which require that the body move forward-backward and from side-to-side in various rolling and locomotor activities.

Examples of some of these activities follow.

Arm-Leg Integration
Modified jumping jacks, in standing positions . . .

Both arms moving, with legs together and jumping . . .

Arm and leg on one side, apart and close to the body . . .

Both arms and legs apart and together at the same time . . .

Practice of this kind can be aided if the child is permitted to watch himself in a mirror.

Using a trampoline gives the child additional time to integrate arm-leg movements, but imposes additional anxiety, and the need for good stability as the bed of the trampoline is contacted.

Arm-leg interactions may be done in a horizontal plane, in a back-lying position. Both arms, moving at once, arms and legs on the same side, arms and legs moving together.

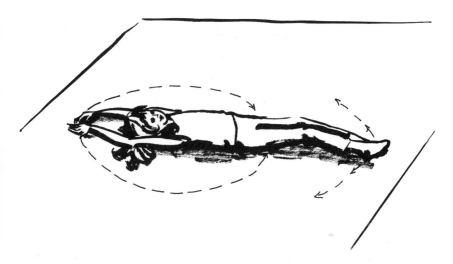

Additional complexity can be gained by asking these movements in the mat to be performed either slowly or rapidly.

Up-Down Activities In a Fixed Position

Getting up and down may be done in various ways . . . to the back, front, side, slowly, and rapidly . . . in various combinations.

Turn and get down, up, etc., can be done in various combinations and in reaction to various left-right directions.

Jumping up and turning to the left or right can be accomplished in various ways, specific jumping practice should be engaged in, helping the child to lift his arms as his legs extend.

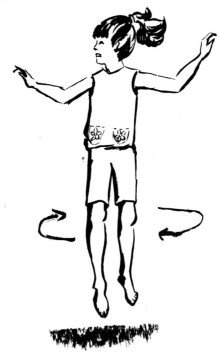

Increased difficulty can be imposed if the jumps and turns are made over low obstacles, or the landings are on the same or different foot than the take-off.

Children should be taught to land properly when jumping from various heights.

Traveling Agility
Axis of the body near the mat and horizontal.

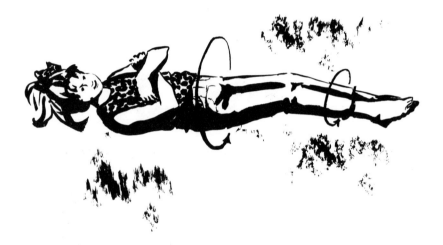

Various rolling movements can be accomplished.

Log rolling in various combinations.

From all fours to all fours.

Rolling in a ball, clasping the knees, using various axes of the body.

Rolling down-hill, individually.

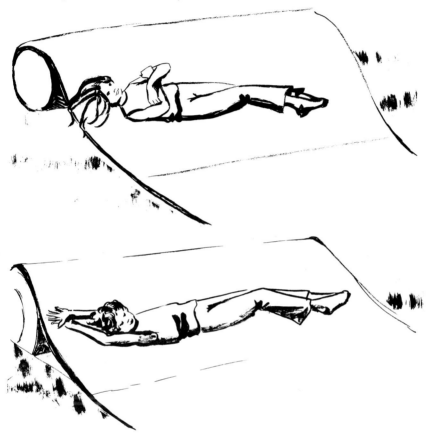

Or in pairs.

Locomotor Agility

Skills which require close visual control should be incorporated into the child's program.

Crawling, requiring that the child place his hands into handprints.

Walking, requiring placement of feet into footprints.

Jumping forward over lines . . . and sideways.

Hopping forward, and sideways.

Jumping backwards.

Hopping backwards.

Skipping and galloping.

BALL HANDLING SKILLS

Throwing. Simple lead-up drills, using only arm movements, and leg-body shift separately might precede throwing movements using both arm and leg movements . . . later practice may be obtained using a ball.

Arm movements only.

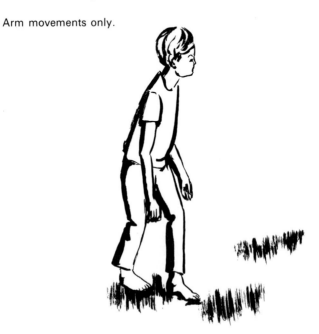

Leg-weight shift only.

A tipping platform may be used.

Arm and leg-weight shift without ball.

Arm-leg-weight shift with ball.

Increased accuracy in placement of ball on vertical and horizontally placed targets.

Vertical

Horizontally placed targets.

Ball Catching. Again lead-up activities should be used. Ball catching becomes harder, of course, when the ball is thrown faster, the ball used is smaller or when its pathway through space is unpredictable from one trial to the next.

Ball rolling.

Watching, touching, and later attempting to catch balls swinging on strings.

Left-to-right.   Near-to-far.

In circles around the child.

In circles in front of the child.

In various planes with the child in a back-lying position.

Left-to-right in a back lying position is more difficult than:

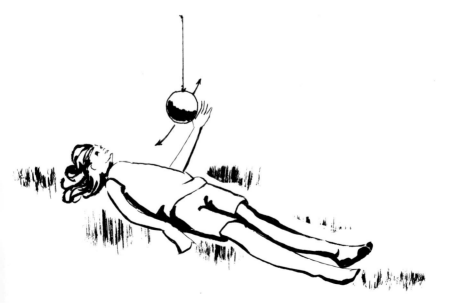

From head-to-foot.

Ball may be bounced . . . first larger ones.

And later thrown from a wide variety of angles.

Batting Balls. A sequence of activities leading toward striking a ball with a bat has been found to be helpful when attempting to improve the skill of inept children within our program at the University of California at Los Angeles. Initially, the child may be asked to hit with a bat a rolled or fixed volleyball on the ground in front of him.

Next he may be asked to hit a volleyball fixed on a batting "T."

The volleyball may be bounced to him for additional difficulty.

Finally, the volleyball may be thrown to him, followed by trials in which balls of decreasing size are used, if he is successful in hitting the larger one.

A recently completed unpublished study carried out in our laboratory clinic at the University of California at Los Angeles involved 65 children* in which the attributes discussed in this chapter were evaluated twice, before and after a five-month program of motor training lasting for two one-hour periods each week (Tuesday–Thursday or Monday–Wednesday). The following changes occurred in the mean scores of the tests used (see Appendix, page 194).

1. The gross agility evidenced significant improvement, pre test mean was 8.07 (SD = 1.92), while the post test mean was 8.65 (t = 2.49). Thus, the children appeared to have gained significant improvement in the attribute necessary to move the body up and down in various ways in simple tumbling movements inherent in the tests. The improvement within this period was greater than that expected during a five-month period upon consulting norms obtained in this test (improvement of children in clinic program was .58 points, improvement expected due to maturation is .31 points).

2. The balancing ability of children similarly improved, based upon the measure of static balance utilized in the battery described. Pre-test mean was 5.48 (SD = 2.29), while the post-test mean was 6.39 (SD = 2.59) (t = 3.81). Improvement expected due to maturation during a five-month period would be .23 points in this test, while this experimental group improved .91 points during this time interval.

3. Locomotor ability similarly improved significantly. The test involves the ability to jump and to hop accurately on mats and with precision into squares. The method of scoring this test is found in the Appendix, page 188. Pre-test mean was 6.54 (SD = 1.81) while post-test mean was 7.74 (SD = 2.07) (t = 2.55). During a five-month period, the improvement expected due to maturation would be about .36 points on this test, while the group participating in this program improved 1.20 points.

4. The ball-handling abilities of the 65 children also improved significantly. A score obtained from the throwing section of the battery referred to changed from a mean of 4.30 (SD = 1.82) to 5.04 (SD = 2.25) (t = 3.43). While the score on the tracking portion of the test battery similarly improved significantly from a mean of 6.22 (SD = 2.23), to a mean of 7.39 (SD = 2.67), (t = 3.71). The improvement in these two tests scores which would be expected due to maturation during a five-month interval would be throwing, .37 points and tracking, .36 points. However, the children described, participating in the program of skill improvement, increased .74 points in throwing and 1.17 points in their ability to watch and to intercept balls.

It is thus apparent from these data that indeed these attributes in children may be changed. The manner in which subtle or obvious transfer occurs between these

---

*The children had been referred from a number of medical, school, and clinical sources as evidencing skill problems. Most were having difficulty in school and evidenced minimal neurological impairment when subjected to neurological examinations. Seven were girls while 58 were boys, a not unusual ratio to be found within a population of children with perceptual-motor problems. The mean age of the group was 8.92 years (SD = 2.48). A control group is presently being tested so that more valid inferences may be made from the data.

attributes and other components of the child's personality is being subjected to further study in our laboratory and in others throughout the country.

SUMMARY

The improvement of control of the larger muscles in the body should include tasks intended to improve balance, agility, ball-handling skills and the like. Such tasks should be presented in a carefully planned sequential manner, from the simple to the more difficult, as the child's ability dictates.

Research indicates that a program containing the activities described in this chapter will elicit a significant improvement in the basic motor attributes of children. Special efforts should be made to include a variety of balance activities, encouraging the improvement of both static and moving balance, locomotor agility, as well as general bodily agility and ball-throwing as well as ball-catching skills.

The activities contained in this chapter should be modified as the instructor assesses the individual needs of his students.

REFERENCES

1. Cratty, Bryant J.: *Developmental Sequences of Perceptual-Motor Tasks-Movement Activities For Neurologically Handicapped And Retarded Children and Youth,* Freeport, L.I., Educational Activities, Inc., 1967.
2. Ismail, A. H. and Gruber, J. J.: *Motor Aptitude and Intellectual Performance,* Columbus, Ohio, Charles E. Merrill, 1968.

9

Music and Rhythm

To an increasing degree, music and various rhythmic activities are being employed in educational programs for atypical children. In one program of perceptual-motor training, for example, all movements are executed to a beat. Music therapy has become a common part of programs for the education of the atypical and the emotionally disturbed.

Music is utilized in two primary ways: (*a*) attempts are made to have children react to and conform to various kinds of beats. This may be accomplished by using some kind of visual and/or sound as stimuli. (*b*) Music may provide a rhythmic background for various types of perceptual-training regimens.

The research outlining the influence of music and rhythmic activity have upon other attributes may be grouped into several categories. The effects of programs of music therapy upon atypical children and adults have been studied by some. Others have investigated the manner in which a rhythmic accompaniment aids the learning of motor skills by normal children. One interesting line of research has begun to elucidate possible links between rhythmic ability and certain academic skills.[20, 21]

Many of the earlier studies purporting to outline the benefits of music therapy were more anecdotal than scientific in nature.[1, 6, 8, 13, 14, 22] In general, it was found that atypical and emotionally disturbed children become more outgoing, more aware of their environment, and more proficient in speech and in motor skills. The greatest success in such programs was realized when children were "bombarded" by rhythmic activities using a number of sensory inputs including visual displays of flags and sounds.[18]

More recent investigations have confirmed, more scientifically, the worth of music as therapy. Fitzpatrick,[5] for example, found improvement in tasks of manual dexterity when the music was coupled with a voice familiar to his adult subjects. Harrison and others[10] similarly found that music, when combined with exercises, exerted a significant positive effect upon various manual skills including buttoning buttons of various sizes, and in reactions to verbal commands such as "sit down," "pick up a ball," etc. This latter program lasted twenty minutes a day, five days a week for a period of four weeks. In both these latter two studies, attempts were made to obtain exact performance measures and control groups were used.

Other researchers have found that teaching motor activities of a rhythmic nature, *i.e.,* swimming, playing musical instruments may exert a significant positive effect upon performance and learning.[4]

Others have attempted to link rhythmic ability to reading. Sterritt and Rudnick completed two studies which indicate that rhythmic ability may exert some influence upon early attempts to read by 1st grade children. By the time a child reaches the third grade, however, factors other than the ability to fragment time into rhythmic patterns influence reading ability, according to these researchers.[20, 21] These studies, however, merely suggest relationships, they do not prove that training in rhythmic tasks will cause reading to improve. Further research may, however, provide evidence that rhythmic training of various kinds aids speech, writing, and reading, all of which may require rhythmic perception.

One important influence upon a child's ability to copy rhythmic patterns is the "natural" preferences he evidences in various tasks in which he is asked to demonstrate his habitual tapping speed, walking speed, and the like. Research by Rimoldi[17] and others,[9] reviewed by Cratty,[3] indicates that certain "personal tempos" are relatively consistent from time to time, within the same part of the body; but at the same time, relative specific to various parts of the body of the same individual. For example, it is not valid to say that an individual is "naturally slow moving" in a general way since an individual's walking speed is usually not predictable upon knowing his preferred speed for leg tapping. On the other hand, the speed and tempo he prefers in a finger tapping task will usually remain reasonably constant when sampled over a period of time.

Thus, when we ask a child to duplicate a rhythmic pattern in some way, his inclination and ability to do so is probably influenced to some degree by the speed he would have *preferred* to move, without any external stimuli present. Thus, some children may be seen who resist moving rapidly in a given task, despite the characteristics of the music and "beat" they are to duplicate, while others may move too rapidly despite a slow tempo to which they are exposed.

Some emotionally disturbed children, blind youngsters, and retardates evidence inappropriate rocking, slapping, and other similar behaviors. Although the genesis of these movements are not well understood, several reasons have been hypothesized for these "blindisms", including the suggestion that they are a method of self-stimulation or that they heighten the body-awareness of the child. In most cases, however, these types of rhythmic movements interfere with the child's ability to learn, to relate to more appropriate stimuli, and with his ability to interact socially with well-adjusted peers and parents. Thus, while in some children it may be attempted to aid them to *establish* rhythmic patterns in movement, others would profit from an *elimination* or *diminution* of extraneous rhythmic activity.

It must be remembered that a given type of rhythmic stimuli (music, visual demonstration, etc.) may have varying effects upon children, exciting some and calming others. Rhythmic activities may, due to lack of concordance with preferred tempos, be difficult for them to engage in. Special care should be taken to present rhythmic activities in progressions to children with learning problems, varying the nature and speed of the stimuli, and the complexity of the reaction expected of the child in reasonable ways condusive to effective learning.

In the pages which follow, several types of rhythmic sequences are presented. Several important considerations should be kept in mind when devising rhythmic activities for children with learning difficulties. The intensity of the stimuli should vary within optimum limits; a noise too loud or too soft will not have the desired effect. The complexity of the stimuli should be arranged in order of difficulty; attempting to react to an uneven beat is more difficult than reacting in some way to a beat separated by equal time intervals.

A third primary consideration involves just what kind of reaction the child is expected to make. Some so-called rhythmic responses are really extremely complex tasks. Hopping alternately first on one foot and then on the other, for example, involves balance and agility as well as the ability correctly to perceive an auditory pattern of sound or a visual demonstration and correctly translate it into corresponding movement patterns. Making rhythmic movements with the hand, on the other hand, may not involve balance and the same complex bodily adjustments.

At the same time, rhythmic patterns in which more than one part of the body is involved are more complicated than tempos in which only one limb is moved. While most difficult are complex movement patterns, seen in some modern dances, in which various tempos are simultaneously replicated in several parts of the body. To some, rhythm is the essence of movement, seen in most of life's natural activities. However, research findings suggesting in exact ways helpful principles concerning just how it is best to incorporate rhythmic movement and music into perceptual-motor education programs properly are not available. The guidelines which follow are recommendations, whose worth may or may not be substantiated by needed studies.

SEQUENCES

Body Part Involvement.   Rhythmic patterns may be translated into movements of various body-parts as the child is seated.

Rhythmic arm movement of the preferred arm with the other arm and legs immobile is probably easiest.

Next in order of difficulty could be expected to be rhythmic movement of the preferred leg to a steady beat of moderate tempo.

Alternate movement of the arms, to a steady tempo is probably next in order of difficulty.

Alternate movement of the legs, while seated, may prove to be more difficult.

Next in order of difficulty is alternate arm-leg action on one side, followed by arm-leg movements made together on the other side of the body.

Finally, movements which involve first one arm, the second arm, and then the legs, one at a time, will prove more difficult. Essentially, the movement "travels" from arm to arm, and then from leg to leg, and back again to the first arm.

Movements which travel diagonally from arm to opposite leg, and then to the second arm, and then to the second leg are most difficult.

Alternate Hopping Movements.   Alternate hopping patterns are difficult for most normal children from five to eight years to execute as explained in Chapter 5, page 54. Thus, to expect neurologically impaired children to execute various hopping movements in which a movement "travels" from leg to leg as they stand may be unrealistic.

Rhythmic walking and skipping movements may be enhanced by first performing these stationary hopping patterns, after first learning these patterns while seated. Following this, rhythmic hopping may be accomplished as the child holds to the back of a chair to increase his stability; and finally, when various hopping patterns have been mastered in this way, he may be asked to hop or to skip without any support. Research has indicated that the following temporal patterns represent a reasonable order of difficulty for this kind of task.[12]

It is easiest to hop alternately three times on one foot and then three times on the other. In a recent study, it was found that about 60 per cent of a group of eight-year-old boys were able to accomplish this movement pattern.[12]

Next in order of difficulty is a pattern involving two hops on one foot and then two on the other. Only about 50 per cent of children eight years old could accomplish this without hesitation, while only about 35 per cent of seven year olds could properly execute this pattern.[12]

The most difficult kind of rhythmic hopping task (and) probably most difficult when alternate arm movements are employed alone) is one in which an uneven number of hops are taken on one foot as compared to the other. A three-two tempo, for example, was found to be executed well only by about 30 per cent of a group of eight year olds, while only about 10 per cent of a group of seven year olds could copy a demonstration of this kind of movement pattern.[12]

Complexity of Stimuli. Research by Bérges and Lézine[2] concerning the imitation of gestures, as well as other studies afford some insight into the way in which the nature and the complexity of the demonstration may influence the manner in which a child can duplicate a pattern in movement.

Easiest are reactions to even tempos involving both visual and auditory stimuli presented at the same time. The vivid flag waving indigenous to the splendid program outlined by Robins,[18] for example, can be expected to elicit the attention of a severely retarded child who is often out of contact with his environment. The flags are heard rippling as they are moved rapidly, at the same time, their bright colors and their movements tend to hold his attention. Thus, he may begin, slowly at first, to react to this type of intense stimuli entering his consciousness through several sensory "channels" at the same time.

Some children may react better to visual stimuli than to sound cues. It will usually be easier for a retarded child to copy a single demonstrated limb movement, than to imitate simultaneously presented rhythmic movements or more than one limb.

This type of imitation will become easier if the child's attempts at movement result in an auditory cue. The well-conceived program evolved by Carl Orff[16] is one of several in which a "rhythm band" is used.

SUMMARY

In general, the following guidelines should be followed when attempting to evolve a program of rhythmics for children.

1. Reasonable sequences should be used in which responses and/or stimuli are arranged in order of difficulty.

2. Since music and rhythmics may either excite or calm children, the tempo and intensity of the stimuli used should be selected so that it brings a child's arousal level closer to the average, *i.e.,* distractible children should be exposed to less intense stimuli, and to slower beats, while lethargic children should be exposed to tempos and stimuli which will raise their level of excitation.

3. As children attend in unpredictable ways to various types of stimuli, visual as well as auditory stimuli, alone or in combinations, should be used when working with children difficult to "reach."

4. Various speeds should be employed. Attempts should be made to present stimuli at speeds comparable with the child's personal tempos, as well as to "break" a child "out" of habitual movement speeds. Flexibility of rhythm should be a goal.

REFERENCES

1. Alvin, J.: "The Response of Severely Retarded Children To Music," *Am. J. Ment. Defic.; 63,* 988–996, 1959.

2. Berges, J. and Lezine, L.: *The Imitation of Gestures,* Spastics Society Medical Education and Information Unit Association, London, William Heinemann, Medical Books, Ltd., 1965.

3. Cratty, Bryant J.: "Personal Equations in Movement," Chapter 12, *Movement Behavior and Motor Learning,* 2nd Ed., Philadelphia, Lea & Febiger, 197–207, 1967.

4. Dillon, Evelyn K.: "A Study of The Use of Music As an Aid In Teaching Swimming," *Res. Quart.; 23,* 1–8, 1952.

5. Fitzpatrick, F. K.: "The Use of Rhythm in Training Severely Subnormal Patients," *Am. J. Ment. Defic.; 63,* 981–987, 1959.

6. Fraser, L. W.: "Music Therapy For the Retarded Child," *Music Therapy,; 6,* 55, 1955.

7. Goldsmith, Carolyn,; "The Use of Rhythmic Patterning For Neurologically Handicapped Children," Reprint 102 from *Academic Therapy Quarterly;* 1–2, DeWitt Reading Clinic, San Rafael, California.

8. Harbert, W. K.: "Some Results From Specific Techniques in the Use of Music With Exceptional Children," *Music Therapy; 2,* 133, 1955.

9. Harrison, R. and Dorcus, R.: "Is Rate of Voluntary Bodily Movements Unitary?," *J. Gen. Psychol.; 18,* 31–39, 1938.

10. Harrison, Wade, Lecrone, J., Temerlin, M. K., and Rousdale, W.: "The Effect of Music and Exercise Upon the Self-Help Skills of Non-Verbal Retardates," *Am. J. Ment. Defic.;* 279–282, 71, 1966.

11. Keller, Wilhelm: "Lecture on Orff-Schulwerk Around the World," Delivered at the First International Symposium on Orff-Schulwerk in the United States, May 2, 1967. (Bellflower City Schools, California).

12. Keogh, Jack F. and Pedigo, P.: "An Evaluation of Performance on Rhythmic Hopping Patterns," Sponsored by National Institute of Child Health and Human Development, UCLA, (Unpublished).

13. Loven, M. S.: "Value of Music Therapy for Retarded Children," *Music Therapy; 6,* 165–171, 1956.

14. Murphy, M. M.: "A Large Scale Music Therapy Program for Institutionalized Low Grade and Middle Grade Defectives," *Am. J. Ment. Defic.; 63,* 268–273, 1958.

15. Nordoff, P. and Robbins, Cline: *"Music therapy for Handicapped Children: Investigations and Experiences,"* New York, Music Publishers Holding Corporation.

16. Orff-Schulwerk: Basic Musical Forms for Orff-Schulwerk Classes in the Elementary School, Mineo. Bellflower School District, Bellflower, California.

17. Rimoldi, H. J. A.: "Personal Tempo," *J. Abn. & Soc. Psychol. 46,* 283–303, 1951.

18. Robins, Ferris, and Robins, Jennet: *Educational Rhythms for Mentally Handicapped Children,* New York, Horizon Press, 1965.

19. Rudnick, Mark, Sterritt, Graham M. and Flax, Morton: "Auditory and Visual Rhythm Perception and Reading Ability," *Child Devel.; 38*–2, 581–587, June, 1967.

20. Sterritt, Graham M. and Rudnick, Mark: "Auditory and Visual Rhythm Perception in Relation to Reading Ability in Fourth Grade Boys," *Percept. & Mot. Skills; 22,* 859–864, 1966.

21. ——: "Reply to Birch and Belmont," *Percept. & Mot. Skills; 23,* 632, 1966.

22. Weigl, V.: "Functional Music: Therapeutic Tool in Working With the Mentally Retarded," *Am. J. Ment. Defic.; 63,* 672–678, 1959.

10

Self-Confidence, the Body-Image, and Game Preferences

A child's total self-concept is a collection of feelings about many things. One component of the child's self includes the manner in which he views his capacities to perform motor tasks. Basic to physical performance, of course, is his "vehicle" for movement, his body.

It is common to find a larger percentage of boys among populations of children with skill problems. For the male in particular, the manner in which he moves in sports situations and his physique represent important variables influencing his self-confidence.

The female, particularly in late childhood and early adolescence, usually has marked feelings about the conformations of her body. Her developing figure, and the extent to which it conforms to acceptable norms are of vital importance to her. It thus seems that for both males and females, whether atypical in some way or normal, the body, its performance capacities and physical characteristics, represents important components of their total self-concept.

In the pages which follow, several facets of a child's self-concept are explored. Literature is reviewed and operational practices recommended which pertain to the body-image, the components of the self-concept having to do with physical performance and appearance, aspiration level as well as the children's perceptions of games they like to play. Game choice, stated opinions of performance potential, as well as measurable aspects of the body-image are inter-related in both obvious and subtle ways. Some of these relationships are explored in the pages which follow, while the elucidation of others awaits further research.

THE BODY-IMAGE

Within recent years, the body-image concept has appeared in literature encompassing a number of disciplines. To some writers, it is a key through which the total self-concept may be appraised; to others it is assessable by merely asking the child to point to various body parts. The methods of evaluation include verbal responses to directions, pointing to body parts, constructing mannikins out of disconnected body parts, drawing pictures of people, self-report questionnaires of various kinds, the imitation of gestures, and projective tests. The application of these measures requires reasonably sophisticated subjects, conditions usually not found within populations of younger children. *

Using the results of assessment devices in which children were asked to respond to various verbal directions, sequences appeared to evolve reasonably which offer guidelines when attempting to enhance the body-image at the verbal-cognitive level. It is obvious, however, that in a more general way, the body-image develops far earlier than does speech and verbal comprehension in both retardates and normal children so that a variety of movement experiences contribute to the development of the body-image in subtle ways.

For example, in a recent study by Hill and others,[12] it was found that various concepts involving the body-image were enhanced equally in two groups of children, one of which received training in which verbal directions involving left-right judgments were included ("throw the ball with your left hand"), as in the other group who were given movement activities involving one hand or foot in which no special verbal directions involving left and right, up and down, etc. were included (*i.e.,* "throw the ball with *this* hand").

Further evidence that movement aids the development of concepts about the body are contained in a study reported by Ilg and Ames,[14] in which it was found that when children were able to make correct left-right judgments of hands, feet, etc., and then were asked *how* they knew their left from their right, they usually attached some motor function to the hand (*i.e.,* "I eat with my right hand", "I write with my left hand", etc.).

Principles evolving from the sensory-tonic theory of perception outlined by Werner and Wapner, suggest that certain alterations of bodily tonus may influence some judgments in visual space.[27] * In laboratory experiments, for example, it is sometimes found that when children's bodies are tilted to the left or to the right, this tends to influence accuracy of their judgments in visual space.[25] However, as normal children get older, they are less likely to be influenced by experimental disruptions of bodily tonus.[25]

The child's body build may influence personality. Kagan, for example found that impulsivity was more often seen in boys whose body builds were made for more vigorous movement (*i.e.,* broader chests, shorter and more muscular bodies). Tall narrow boys, on the other hand, were found to be more reflective than active in nature.[15] Generally, normal adults and children know what common physique-personality stereotypes consist of,[21] and may tend to act accordingly. Investigations of personality-physique comparisons among retarded children, to our knowledge, have not been carried out. However, with further study, it is possible that causal relationships may be discovered, which will lead to more meaningful

---

*A recent summary of methods in which the body-image may be evaluated is contained in a monograph by Cratty and Sams.[8]

*A critical evaluation of this theory has been written by Howard and Templeton.[13]

motor education programs for children in which body-image modifications might lead toward desirable personality trait changes. For example, the thin insecure child may be aided to achieve greater self-confidence by the addition of muscle to his vulnerable body-frame via exercise. As the result of several studies using normal, blind, and retarded subjects, we have evolved various sequences of body-image judgments. Summarized, the following guidelines are apparently helpful in the evaluation and training of the body-image.

1. Simple judgments about parts of the face and location and names of the limbs should constitute the initial portion of a body-image training program for immature children. Models of the face and drawings of the child's body are helpful during this phase.

2. In conjunction with this initial phase, children should also begin to obtain simple object-to-body relationships (place the body nearest your head, your feet, your side, your stomach, your back). More difficult are judgments in which the child has to re-arrange his body, and react correctly to "place your side against the wall, lie down on your back," etc.

3. Simple directions involving body movements should next be given, including total movement of the body ("move to the side, forward, backward, jump up, squat down") as well as limb movements. Imitative exercises, using a teacher-model, as well as a mirror (*i.e.,* "swing your arms", "bend your knees" etc.), are helpful in this stage.

4. Difficulty can be added to exercises within these initial three phases by chaining directions together, *i.e.,* "jump down and turn around", etc.

5. When a child is about six, he should be exposed to body-image activities intended to enhance his knowledge of left and right. Many left-right things should be done during this phase, including movements, pointing to body parts, etc. Easiest are activities in which the child remains fixed and is asked to touch various left-right body parts. Next in order of difficulty are judgments in which he must place objects to his left or right; and finally most difficult are those in which he has to re-orient himself in various left-right ways, *i.e.,* "place your left side nearest the wall, turn to your left, etc."

6. Concurrently, the child should be taught that space has left-right dimensions which correspond to his body-parts, and, operationally, transfer from body to space should be taught (*i.e.,* "See John, the letter D faces toward your right hand, stretch your hand out and touch it, do you understand?").

7. Judgments of the left and right of another person are usually possible by eight or nine years.

Various activities may be engaged in which aid a child to gain an awareness of his body size, and the relative size of body parts. Kephart has suggested that doing a "seat-drop" when trampolining will aid a child to compare his total body height to upper body size. Drawing outlines around children as they lie on shelf paper or while they are standing against a blackboard, and then having them inspect these may aid a child to form a more accurate awareness of his body size. Gottsman[10] and others have devised tests which use the selection of body silhouettes in an effort to evaluate an individual's perceptions of his own bodily conformations.[10] It is apparent that judgments about the location of body parts, the body's left-right dimensions, bodily movements, and the perception of body size are all important components of a body-image training program for children. It is equally obvious, upon surveying the literature, that a primary way in which these percepts and concepts may be obtained is through carefully sequenced movement experiences.

THE PERFORMING "SELF"

In addition to perceptions about body size and the location of body parts, an important component of the child's self-concept is related to what he can *do* with his body. Two types of approaches concerning the evaluation of a child's concept of his "performing self" have been posited. Various measures of aspiration level may be made concerning expected performance in a *specific task** or less exact self-reports may be collected concerning how a child *generally* feels about himself in a variety of performance situations ("Are you clumsy?").

In general, studies of aspiration level compare estimates of performance with actual performance on trials of a given task. The findings from these studies usually confirm common observations: (a) subjects with a background of success tend to aspire to better performance; (b) continued failure elicites low estimates of future performance; (c) insecure individuals over-react to failure and to success *i.e.,* aspiring too highly after doing well, and too low after performing poorly.

We have used a survey form involving self-reports to assess children's self-opinions of motor performance and physical appearance in a more general way. This type of form is not recommended unless the child is about seven or eight years old.* A score is obtained by direct yes-no answers to such questions as "are you clumsy?", "are you the last to be chosen in games?", "are you good at making things with your hands?", etc. (A complete copy of the form is contained in the Appendix, page 214). The over-all score is obtained from the number of negative responses to this type of question. The results of a pre-post test comparison administered to 65 children (mean age = 8.9 years) bracketing a motor education program lasting five months are as follows.

1. In the pre-test, the children's responses were most likely to reflect negative self-concepts in statements suggesting that their friends make fun of them, that they are having trouble making friends, that they are the last to be chosen in games, that the opposite sex does not like them, and that in games they watch instead of play (Statements numbered 5, 7, 11, 12, and 15, See Appendix, page 214).

2. In the post-test, their answers reflected the same degree of negativism (See results, page 214 in Appendix).

It became apparent to us upon reviewing these data that although the performance scores of these children changed significantly, their feelings about this performance apparently had not. It suggests that individuals assuming to heighten a child's concept of himself through improvement in motor activities take special

*A review of some of these studies using motor performance measures may be found in *Social Dimensions of Physical Activity,* Chapter III, Aspiration Level[7] (Prentice-Hall, Inc. 1967).
*A short-form of a test developed by Piers and Harris and used with their permission.[17]

steps to inform the child of his improvement in very concrete and direct ways. The child, for example, should be shown graphs illustrating improvements in tasks.

Several other explanations may be made for these findings. (*a*) The children during the second testing felt more at ease and thus more readily admitted negative feelings about themselves; (*b*) Improvement in the clinic program had not transferred to real life situations for the child and/or (*c*) his answers do not reflect his true feelings.

Very important to most young children is the degree to which they can do something. It is the feeling they have about how they perform in obvious ways which is likely to exert positive or negative influence upon their total self-concept. It is thus important to survey children's general and specific feelings about their potential to perform a number of tasks, prior to devising programs of motor training purporting to change their performance concept.* Sometimes this evaluation can be carried out in a relatively simple manner, by simply asking a child how far he can execute a standing broad jump, prior to jumping; and then asking for further estimates after the first trial. If the child refuses to guess or makes a gross over-estimation, it may be assumed that there is some distortion in his "motor" self-concept. If the child refuses to adjust to reality, there is cause for concern, *i.e.*, when after an under-or-over-estimation he refuses to be influenced by the distance jumped on the previous performance trial when making his next estimate. A child whose concept of his performance potential is extremely low must be placed initially in situations in which he receives continual success experiences, whereas a child whose opinion of his performance potential is not as low may be challenged to a greater degree.

GAME CHOICE

Several measures of children's choices of games they prefer to play have been utilized in research.[18,22,23] At times, these tests purport to measure gender identification in children. One of the most used measures of this type was developed by Rosenberg and Sutton-Smith.[22] We have used a modification of this test to evaluate the vigor of the activities children preferred prior to and following a program of motor education conducted at the University of California at Los Angeles. In addition, norms using this particular test were obtained from a school district using 604 children from grades 2 through 5. A summary of the findings of this research is as follows:

1. As the children grew older, they tended to select fewer games from the list. For example, the girls in the 2nd grade selected from 16 to 18 games they liked to play, but when the children in the 4th and 5th grades were polled (nine and ten year olds), they proved to be more selective and chose, on the average, 8 games.

2. A survey of the weighted scores given to the various games revealed that significant differences were elicited from both sexes by the 2nd grade (seven year olds).

*It may be found that a considerable difference exists between actual performance measured and the child's feelings about his performance.

(A detailed summary of the norms are found in the Appendix, pages 211, 212).

It might be assumed, therefore, that a boy with motor problems, withdrawing from active games given value by his male peers, and gravitating toward the games in which the girls participate, will begin to evidence significant shifts in scores on this type of games-choice test. Thus, a comparison was made of the number and type of games selected by normal children to those same measures collected from 64 children with movement problems. The results of this comparison are as follows:

1. There appeared to be no significant difference in the "masculine" scores elicited from 57 boys with motor problems, and 82 nine-year-old boys upon whom this modified Sutton-Smith had been normed. Mean for the "motor problem" group was 29.00 (SD = 14.00), and for the norms of 26.64 (SD = 4.85) (t = 1.21).

2. At the same time, the 57 boys with motor problems tended to also select a significantly larger number of feminine games they preferred to play, as contrasted to the 82 nine-year-old boys upon whom this test was normed. The mean "feminine" game choice score by the boys with motor problems (mean age of 8.90 years) was 18.52 (SD = 15.00), whereas the mean feminine score on the part of a normal population of 82 boys was 4.85 (SD = 6.51) (t = 6.41).

It appears, therefore, that boys with skill problems may, while making "correct" masculine choices when presented with such a list, tend also to play a significantly larger number of "feminine" games than do boys without skill problems.

Summarized results of previous studies in which this measure and others have been utilized, are as follows.

1. Boys and girls game choices tend to be similar up until the age of seven and eight, at which time the girls tend to choose more passive activities, and the boys the more active.

2. Through the years, girls in America have tended to evidence an increased tendency to select vigorous games at earlier ages, based upon comparisons of game choices using the same measure taken twenty years apart.[23]

3. Game choice is only one of the indices that improper gender identification may be occurring in a given child. Others include the inclination to use gestures like a member of the opposite sex, expressing the desire to be a member of the opposite sex, and dressing like a member of the opposite sex.

4. As a child matures, he tends to become more selective when confronted with lists of games; he tends to pick fewer as he grows older.

Children's behavior patterns tend to be transmitted from one to the other. Thus it is possible that a boy refused participation in vigorous games may tend to select the more passive games in which girls participate, and, as a result, begin to imitate their gestures and other movement characteristics.

Although there are no definitive studies on this point of which we are aware, it is apparent to many educators upon observing groups of boys with skill problems that there is sometimes an excess of evasive and silly behavior within the group. It is possible that introduction of vigorous activity, accompanied by specific training in movement patterns which are generally seen among boys (vigorous striking with a fist, a wide base when running, etc.), might aid such boys to achieve better acceptance by their peers when at play.

12

SUMMARY

A child's total feelings about himself are composed of both obvious and subtle components, some of which relate to and/or are influenced by motor activity and motor attributes. On the previous pages, some of these related components were discussed, including the body-image, body-size, general self-confidence in motor activity, as well as aspiration level in specific tasks and game choice. More important than how a child performs is how he *feels* about his performance when it is completed, and what, if anything, he chooses to do next. Cognizance of the importance of these feelings by individuals attempting to enhance the total development of atypical children through motor activity should make their efforts more successful.

REFERENCES

1. Aarts, J. F. M. C.: "Some Experiments on The Accuracy of Self-Judgements," *Arto. Psychol.; 25,* 137–158, 1966.
2. Adams, N. and Caldwell, W.: "The Children's Somatic Apperception Test," *J. Gen. Psychol.; 68,* 43–57, 1963.
3. Berges, J. and Lezine, L.: *The Imitation of Gestures,* The Spastics Society Medical Education and Information Unit Association, London, William Heinemann, Medical Books Ltd., 1965.
4. Clausen, Johannes: *Ability Structure and Subgroups in Mental Retardation,* Washington, Spartan Books, 1966.
5. Cratty, Bryant J.: *Developmental Sequences of Perceptual-Motor Tasks: Movement Activities for Neurologically Handicapped and Retarded Children and Youth,* Freeport, L.I., New York, Educational Activities, Inc., 1967.
6. ———: *Perceptual-Motor Attributes of Mentally Retarded Children and Youth* (Monograph), Los Angeles County Mental Retardation Services Board, 1966.
7. ———: *Social Dimensions of Physical Activity,* Englewood Cliffs, New Jersey, Prentice-Hall, Inc., 1967.
8. Cratty, Bryant J. and Sams, Theressa: *The Body-Image of Blind Children* (Monograph), Sponsored by the American Foundation For the Blind, New York, 1968.
9. Gallagher, James J.: "Measurement of Personality Development in Pre-Adolescent Mentally Retarded Children," *Am. J. Ment. Defic.; 64,* 296–384, Sept., 1959.
10. Gottesman, Eleanor and Brown, L. W.: "The Body-Image Identification Test: A Quantitative Propeture Technique to Study as Aspect of the Body-Image," *J. Genet. Psychol.; 108,* 19–34, 1966.
11. Guyette, A., Wapner, Seymour, Werner, Heinz, and Davidson, John: "Some Aspects of Space Perception in Mental Retardates," *Am. J. Ment. Defic.; 69,* 90–100, July, 1964.
12. Hill, S. D., McCullum, A. A., and Aceau, A.: "Relation of Training In Motor Activity to Development of Left-Right Directionality In Mentally Retarded Children: Exploratory Study," *Percept. & Mot. Skills; 24,* 363–366, 1967.
13. Howard, I. P., and Templeton, W. B.: *Human Spatial Orientation,* New York, John Wiley & Sons, 1966.
14. Ilg, Frances L. and Ames, Louise Bates: *School Readiness,* New York, Harper & Row, 1965.
15. Kagan, Jerome: "Body Build and Conceptual Impulsivity in Children," *J. Person.; 34,* 118–128, 1966.

16. Oliver, J. N.: "The Effect of Physical Conditioning Exercises and Activities On The Mental Characteristics Of Educationally Sub-Normal Boys," *Br. J. Ed. Psychol.: 28,* 155–165, June, 1958.
17. Piers, Ellen V., and Harris, Dale B.: "Age and Other Correlates on Self-Concept In Children," *J. Ed. Psychol.; 55,* April, 1964.
18. Rosenberg, B. G., and Sutton-Smith, B.: "The Measurement of Masculinity and Femininity In Children," *Child. Devel.; 30,* 373–380, 1959.
19. ———: "A Revised Conception of Masculine-Feminine Differences in Play Activities," *J. Genet. Psychol.; 96,* 165–170, 1960.
20. Secord, Paul F., and Jourard, Sidney, M.: "The Appraisal of Body-Cathexis: Body-Cathexis and the Self," *J. Consult. Psychol.; 17,* 343–347, 1953.
21. Sleet, David A.: "Somatotype and Social Image," Paper presented at the Annual Meeting of the California Association of Health, Physical Education, and Recreation; San Jose, California, April 8, 1968.
22. Sutton-Smith, and Rosenberg, B. G.: *Play and Game List,* Bowling Green Ohio: Bowling Green State University, 1959.
23. ———: "Sixty Years of Historical Changes in the Game Preferences of American Children," *J. Am. Folkl.; 74,* 17–46, 1961.
24. Sutton-Smith, B., Rosenberg, B. G., and Morgan, E. F.: "Development of Sex Differences in Play Choices During Pre-Adolescence," *Child Devel.; 34,* 119–126, 1963.
25. Wapner, Seymour and Heinz, Werner: *Perceptual Development: An Investigation Within the Framework of Sensory Tonic Field Theory,* Clark University Press, 1957.
26. Weatherford, R. S. and Harrocks, John: "Peer Acceptance and Over and Under Achievement in School," *J. Psychol.; 66,* 215–220, 1967.
27. Werner, Heinz and Wapner, W.: "Sensory-Tonic Field Theory of Perception," *J. Person.; 18,* 88–107, 1949.
28. Zeaman, D. and House, Betty J.: "The Role of Attention In Retardate Discrimination Learning," In *Handbook of Mental Deficiency,* N. R. Ellis (Ed.), New York, McGraw-Hill Book Co., 159–223, 1963.

11

Games with Ideas

Most children like to play games, particularly if the games involve total movement of the body through space. To an increasing degree, games of this nature are being utilized as channels through which children learn concepts and skills usually associated with the classroom. Jim Humphrey[9] at the University of Maryland has demonstrated that better learning of verbal skills and of arithmetic concepts occurred with some children when they were taken to the playground where mathematical and verbal skills were incorporated into their games than was achieved when using the traditional workbooks.

Schools for special education in the City of Los Angeles have added lines and configurations to the patterns usually found on the playground with the intention to use total body movement as a learning modality in addition to the visual, auditory, and tactual channels ordinarily relied upon. While this method of instructing concepts and classroom skills has several advantages, it is not intended to imply that traditional methods should be replaced by the so-called learning-games.

There are several reasons why movement as a learning modality holds promise for the education of children with learning dificulties, one of which is the strong motivation attached to it. Game performance is a motivating device for many children because the results of their activity are immediate and concrete. It is instantly rewarding for a child to spell a word correctly in some game situation in the classroom or on the playground so that he can proceed to the next base. While movement as a learning modality may not be essential for all children, a study directed by Petri[13] supports the idea that movement can help some children learn.

According to Petri, children deal with their environment in two ways. Some children explore their environment through total body movement, and this group was labeled reducers of stimuli. The second group tends to be very inactive physically, and these children were called the augmenters of stimuli. The reducer prefers moving about in his environment, rather than sitting quietly and perceiving the activity about him. He tends to be less sensitive to pain and to visual stimuli. Further, because of his activity, he tends to inhibit input. The augmenter thus manifests a tendency to absorb information passively and is less inclined to movement.

164

If Petri's hypothesis is accepted, then it would seem that learning methods should be of several types to satisfy the needs of the augmenter and the reducer of stimuli. While the augmenter is receptive to regular classroom teaching techniques, the reducer seems to need a different approach to learning. One type of child, then, learns through passively perceiving his environment, while the other needs movement to stimulate his input system.

Total movement may better demonstrate the quality of a child's thought processes to the observing teacher than will more subtle performance on desk-top tasks. The difficulty of tasks described on the following pages may be easily altered; large stimuli are being reacted to and most of these stimuli may be changed continually to make the tasks challenging.

While many children learn easily and readily respond to the audio-visual stimuli with classroom desk-top work, some very vigorous boys may benefit from a different approach, one in which body movements are included. The boy who attempts to assert his masculinity by engaging in frequent movement may be more amenable to more vigorous learning methodologies than to the passive classroom tasks having a feminine connotation taught by his feminine teacher. Kagan,[11] for example, found that with the possible exception of mathematics, most classroom tasks such as reading and writing are felt to be feminine by boys in the elementary school. Movement tasks oriented toward the acquisition of concepts needed in the classroom may help a hyperactive child improve his motor problems. Well-designed movement tasks may help boys develop self direction and control.

Several classifications of concepts which may be improved through movement activities are discussed in this chapter. Included are tasks purporting to enhance serial memory ability, the recognition of and discrimination between geometric patterns, choice-making behavior, and the ability to classify. Games on grids containing letters and numbers are taught the children as a means of developing spelling and arithmetic skills, as well as simple letter and number recognition. Base games arranged in order of difficulty conclude this section.

SERIAL MEMORY ABILITY

Serial memory ability is an important part of learning. The correct arrangement of letters into words, words into phrases, and the ability to recall a series of instructions in correct order are vital qualities for a child to possess. A close relationship exists between the ability to remember a series of stimuli and the ability to assimilate a number of stimuli at a single exposure (perceptual-span). There are several hypotheses which attempt to explain how components in a series are remembered. Some studies suggest that one item seems to trigger the next item in a series; other research states that the location of a given item in a series is important, while a third assumption is that both these processes interact to aid children remember things in a series and to place them in correct order.[10]

Relating to these projects in serial memory ability, the findings of two studies by Cratty[4,5] have demonstrated that the serial learning of words is in some ways similar to how a series of movements are learned. Movement activities may be used to heighten serial memory in several ways.

1. A single child may watch another child execute the series of movements

and then: (*a*) he may attempt to imitate the series himself (a fairly difficult task); (*b*) he may instruct a third child on the manner in which the first child moved through the various configurations (easier than the first sub-problem recommended).

    2. The instructor may add to the number of "movement items" a given child must do or attempt to imitate. With trainable retardates, it is best to start with one, then move to two, and later to three and four movement sub-tasks; many normal youngsters can remember five, six, and even seven.

    3. Serial memory tasks of the preceding nature may be combined with instructions which encourage the development of other perceptual and conceptual attributes concurrently. For example, these configurations may consist of geometrical figures, of letters, or of combinations of figures and letters. Children seem to find it easier to identify larger geometric figures than smaller ones. Therefore, they can more readily recall the items in a serial memory task if the larger letters and figures are used than to try to identify the smaller letters of a printed page in their books. To stimulate the reader to try some of these learning activities with certain children, a few suggestions are offered.

    A child may be asked to perform some activity to one or more of the patterns, or he may be asked to identify verbally the type of pattern encountered, before proceeding to do some movement within it, over it, or around it. The children who are watching may be asked to call out each geometric shape encountered by the performer as he reaches it.

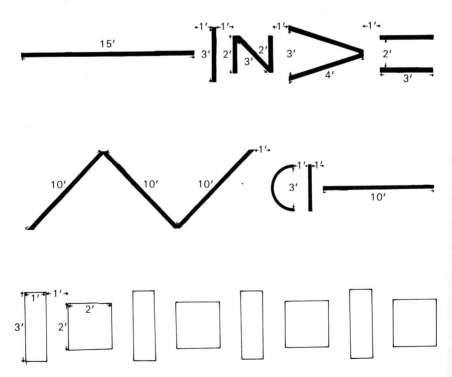

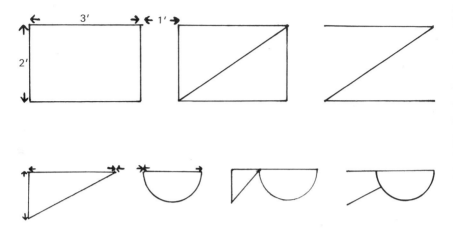

Various kinds of cross-modal transfer problems may be worked out in this situation if a child, for example, is asked to draw each figure he encounters in the serial task on an adjacent blackboard.[14]

Pattern sequences may contain both lines and geometric figures placed in order. In the following diagram, when a child walks the line (1), dynamic balance is aided; when he jumps over the next line (2), visual-motor coordination is required, and when he copies another child in these two movements, serial memory ability is involved. When he encounters the triangle, he may be asked, "What is it?" before being asked to jump into it with his left foot first (pattern recognition and left-right discrimination); and as he gets to the final square, he may be asked to perform in four ways in using the square (decision making).

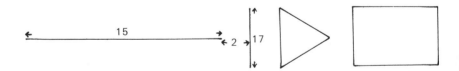

Using the same series of patterns, place one child at each of the four patterns. Ask each child to do four or more movements on, around, or in his pattern. Each of these four performers may be observed by four other children who evaluate their efforts and keep score. Many teachers, after they have given the children a problem to solve, fail to give the children sufficient time to think about what they want to do within the limits of the assigned task. Too frequently teachers expect an immediate response to the assigned problem.

If materials are available, such as obstacle course may be constructed of tires, boxes, and other materials which encourage a child to work in a third dimension, height. As soon as the children are able to engage in this kind of decision making behavior, they should be encouraged to construct their own obstacle course using tape and other available objects.

PATTERN RECOGNITION

In Chapter 3 the idea of the lesson in triangles was discussed. If the triangles were observed, touched, and talked about so that some triangular concept had been formulated, then a triangle lesson using total body movement would make use of another aspect of the child's nature to develop the concept of triangularity (*i.e.,* an enclosed space bounded by three sides, intersecting at three corners). Similar lessons in geometric figures must accompany similar movement tasks on the playground.

A few geometric figures with their dimensions are suggested as guides to what would be appropriate to paint on a playground. Other things such as letters of the alphabet may also benefit some children with problems.

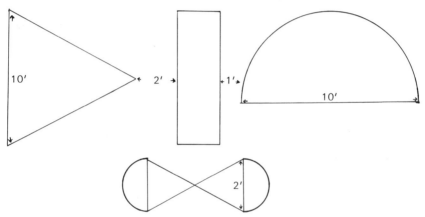

Pattern recognition training can be carried out in a number of ways.

1. Triangles cut out in the classroom may be taken to the playground so that similar patterns may be found inscribed there.

2. Children may be encouraged to trace a triangular (or square or circular) shaped pathway in a sandbox as they walk through it.

3. Various geometric figures may be drawn on a blackboard placed outside and then children may race to the corresponding figures on the playground.

4. Reasonably complex figures may be drawn on a piece of paper, and then the child may be required to walk in a similar pattern in a sandbox. Research by Keogh and Keogh indicates that some children have great dificulty organizing and fragmenting space in this way.[17] Some of the patterns which may be employed in this type of task are:

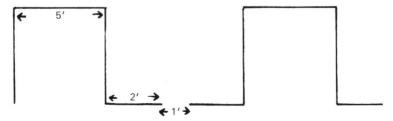

CLASSIFICATION, CATEGORIZATION

Researchers interested in cognitive processes frequently identify the ability to arrange stimuli into classifications as an important attribute underlying thought. Movement tasks properly presented may help some children to learn how to classify. Clarke and others[1] have demonstrated that a remarkable amount of transfer may occur between various tasks in which different stimuli are sorted. A few suggestions may bring out other ideas.

1. To encourage children to arrange movements into categories; request them to demonstrate ways of: (*a*) jumping over a line, (*b*) stepping over a line, (*c*) walking the length of a line.

2. An observing child may attempt to classify the movements of another child into categories of jumping, hopping, rolling, walking, etc., movements, as he watches him deal with the previously described line "obstacle courses" or perhaps rolling movements of various kinds using a mat.

D	A	Y	M	S	U
X	R	U	P	B	G
B	L	K	I	H	Q
M	Z	R	E	F	O
C	O	I	V	M	T
W	D	T	P	V	E

SPELLING, ARITHMETIC

Grids (6 x 6 feet) containing 36 squares (1 x 1 foot) are a helpful way of teaching some children to spell and to handle various simple numerical concepts. The immature child, the child who resists traditional ways of teaching these skills, as well as the vigorous, muscular boy who is more likely to be hyperactive, are all receptive to these kinds of tasks.

The interior of each grid square should be large enough to contain both feet of a reasonably large child. If the size of the total grid is too large, difficulty will be incurred as the child attempts to get from letter to letter as he jumps and spells. Innumerable games may be played utilizing these squares. Care, of course, must be taken so that the child is correctly oriented to the letters and numbers and is not viewing them upside down when asked to identify them.

5	6	5	7	8	4
8	2	6	8	2	3
3	4	1	5	6	7
9	0	3	9	1	0
7	3	4	0	6	1
2	8	2	1	7	9

1. The child may be asked to jump randomly around the squares of the grid; to identify letters or numbers by jumping on them as directed; to spell his name or various words he uses in his writing and reading vocabulary by jumping on letters in sequence.

2. The child may spell words by throwing bean bags into the lettered squares.

3. Two children may be given a single letter and asked to see who can get to the letter first.

4. Words or letters may be flashed to the children who then must duplicate the order by jumping or hopping into the proper squares containing the same words or letters. The same activity may be repeated with the number squares.

5. Children in adjacent squares may race to see who can spell words correctly and finish first by jumping into the appropriate squares.

6. The answers to mathematics problems may be found by having the children compute the answers by jumping into the correct squares.

Some of these activities are illustrated.

Research studying improvement of spelling, arithmetic skills, number recognition and similar skills using these activities is presently underway in our laboratory.

BASE GAMES AND THE USE OF SPACE

Base games are popular with children of all ages. However, to participate successfully in a base game such as kickball, an elementary child must successfully integrate and "call-up", when appropriate, from 10 to 15 simple rules. It is apparent that children with learning problems, then, may not be able to participate successfully in even these low organized games because there are too many rules for them to sort out quickly.

The suggested activities illustrate ways in which lead-up base games may be introduced to the child by developing a sequence of base games, starting with very simple ones and moving toward those that are more complex.

Too much movement in a retarded child's visual space serves to confuse him. He becomes more dismayed if he is required to move too rapidly through moving objects and people. It is important that he is gradually introduced to games that demand more movement of objects and people. The initial games in the series have been selected to keep complex movements to a minimum. For example, if a retarded child is asked to run from base to base within a playfield composed of moving outfielders and the moving ball, he may well "get lost" while attempting to move from second to third base. On the other hand, if the base is placed at a point outside the usual playing field, some of this confusion is dissipated. It is easier for a child to organize the space requirements of a base game if there is no ball involved in the activity during the initial phases of learning. Therefore, the first games are played without a ball, and the child is required to find various bases and to move to them in a given order.

Playing many base games helps the child gain different attributes such as: the keeping of score which helps develop arithmetic skills, and the remembering of the order in which the bases are to be run develops the child's serial memory ability. Various dynamic properties of space and the child's ability to deal with them are learned as balls are intercepted and propelled from player to player.

The sequence of activities below is meant to offer helpful guidelines. Teachers may discover intermediate activities or may modify the games illustrated in any manner that will be helpful to the participating children.

1. 2-BASE
   One, two or more bases may be placed from 10 to 15 feet apart, and as children pass between them, or fun figure-eights around them, they can be asked to tell when their left or right side, or hand, is nearest the nearest base. Modifications can be made in the method of travel, and children can hop, jump, or skip between the bases.

2. 3-BASE TRAVELS

Using three bases placed in a triangle, children can run or move in other ways between the bases, gaining the concept of triangularity, counting bases, and generally locating the bases.

3. 4-BASE CHANGES

Beginning with four children on each of four bases, a fifth "leader" can call "change." Each child attempts to reach the next base by running, jumping, etc. before the other three can. The last child to arrive becomes "out" and a new child joins the other three to play again.

4. 3 OR 4-BASE STAND AND THROW

Using three of four bases, children may stand on each base and throw, roll, or bounce a ball around the bases. Additional stress may be imposed as another child, by running or moving in some other way, attempts to circle the outside of the bases attempting to beat the throw around, as shown in the second illustration.

5. 4-BASE THROW AND RUN TO WIN

The "up" child may kick or hit the ball to the outfield and then may attempt to circle the bases as many times as possible, passing home to first base more than once as he can. Score is kept on how many bases are touched, before the outfield can intercept the ball and stop the runner by lining up, passing the ball to the rear most man who may yell "stop."

6. 1-BASE THROW AND RUN

Using a ball the "up" child may throw, hit or kick a ball to the other children in the outfield. He can then attempt to circle the single base as many times as he can, counting his attempts, before the outfielders can "stop" him by intercepting the ball, lining up behind each other, passing the ball to the rear man who yells "stop" to terminate the actions of the "up" man.

7. 1-BASE CIRCLE YOUR TEAMMATES

After hitting, throwing or kicking the ball, the up man circles his own teammates, while the outfielders all react by lining up behind the man intercepting it, passing it to the rear man who yells "stop" to stop the runner. Activities of this nature in which all of the players have to do something most of the time are helpful in so far as there is less probability that the immature or distractible child will remove his attention from the game situation.

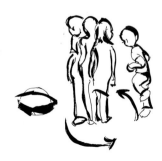

8. 2-BASE HIT AND TRAVEL

The up man kicks, hits or throws the ball, and then travels to the 2nd base which is in a direction *opposite* to that in which the outfielders are located. The outfielders attempt to return the ball home or line up and yell "stop" as described in the previous games before the up man can return to home base again. Two players up can also be used, so that the first player does not have to return home, but may be. "hit" home by the other's efforts. Traveling to bases outside the field of play is helpful insofar as confusion caused by the simultaneous movements of balls, outfielders, and base runners within the same space is reduced. There is less likely to be accidents when this type of modification is employed for children with movement problems.

9. 3-AND 4-BASE HIT, KICK, AND COUNT

The up player propels the ball in some manner to the outfield, and begins to run the bases continuously counting how many he can touch (he may circle them several times) before the outfield can return the ball, line up, and yell "stop", or in some other way terminate his efforts. Only one player at a time need be "up" so that waiting for a turn can be eliminated as all players are in the outfield, when not otherwise occupied. Players may be up several times and the winner is decided by the total bases traversed; thus the game affords counting and adding practice.

10. 4-BASE FORCE HOME

With five or more players on a team, players hit or otherwise propel the ball, and then just run to 1st base, moving ahead one base when their teammate hits the ball. All runs are thus forced home, and only forced outs may be made by touching a base ahead of a base runner. Three outs to a side. This modification eliminates some of the rules found in the ordinary kickball game, and at the same time lessens the chances for injury as players do not hit or tag a runner with the ball.

If and when these games are mastered, the child may be ready for standard games such as kickball. At times, if the teacher attempts to change from game to game too rapidly, negative transfer will occur (*i.e.,* the rules of the previous game will interfere with the learning of subsequent games). It is well to spend some time with a single game and its modifications prior to moving to a second game, particularly if the children involved evidence marked learning problems.

SUMMARY

The learning games outlined on the preceding pages are not presented as ways to replace traditional learning techniques, but as helpful adjuncts to these. The creative teacher should be able continually to make modifications to the tasks outlined if the principles underlying these activities are thoroughly understood.

Activities of this type are a helpful way of observing the quality of a child's thought processes. At various points during the performance of these kinds of skills, the teacher should permit, indeed should encourage, silent contemplation of the elements of the task the child is trying to organize. Sometimes, particularly in the case of the severely retarded, the time required prior to some decision being made may be prolonged indeed. The teacher should attempt to control her own anxieties during this apparently inactive period of time, for what could be more gratifying to a teacher or a parent than to observe a child silently stand and think.

REFERENCES

1. Clarke, Ann, Cooper, G. M. and Henney, A. S.: "Width of Transfer and Task Complexity in the Conceptual Learning of Imbeciles", *Br. J. Psychol.; 57,* 121–128, 1966.
2. Cratty, Bryant J.: "Comparison of Verbal-Motor Performance and Learning in Serial Memory Tasks", *Res. Quart.; 34,* 431–439, December, 1964.
3. ———: *Learning and Playing: 50 Vigorous Games for Atypical Children,* Freeport, New York, Educational Activities, Inc., 1968.
4. ———: "Moving and Learning", Chapter XI, in Developmental Sequences of Perceptual-Motor Tasks, Freeport, New York, Educational Activities, Inc., 1967.
5. ———: "Recency vs. Primary in a complex Gross Motor Task", *Res. Quart.; 34,* 3–8, 1963.
6. Ghent, L., and Bernstein, L.: "Effect of Orientation on Recognition of Geometric Forms by Retarded Children", *Child, Devel.; 35,* 1127–1136, 1963.
7. Gibson, E. J., Gibson, J. J., Pick, A. and Oseer, H. A.: "A Developmental Study of the Discrimination of Letter-Like Forms", *J. Comp. Phys. Psychol.; 55,* 897–907, 1962.
8. Hill, S. D., McCullum, A. H. and Sceau, A.: "Relation of Training In Motor Activity to Development of Left-Right Directionality in Mentally Retarded Children: Exploratory Study", *Percept. & Mot. Skills; 24,* 363–366, 1967.
9. Humphrey, James H.: "Comparison of the Use of Active Games and Language Workbook Exercises as Learning Media in the Development of Language Understandings With Third Grade Children", *Percept. & Mot. Skills; 21,* 23–26, 1965.
10. Jensen, Arthur R. and Rolnver, D. Jr.: "What is Learned in Serial Learning?", *J. Verbal Behavior; 4,* 62–72, 1965.
11. Kagan, J., Wright, J. C. and Bayley, N.: "Psychological Development of the Child", Chapter 12 in *Human Development* Frank Falkner (Ed.), Philadelphia, W. B. Saunders Co., 1966.

12. Keogh, Barbara, K. and Keogh, Jack F.: "Pattern Copying and Pattern Walking Performance of Normal and Educationally Subnormal Boys", *Am. J. Ment. Defic.; 71,* 1009–1013, 1967.

13. Petri, Asenath: *Individuality in Pain and Suffering,* Chicago, University of Chicago Press, 1967.

14. Pick, Ame D., Pick, H. and Thomas, Margaret: "Cross-Model Transfer and Improvement of Form Discrimination: *J. Exp. Child. Psychol.; 3,* 279–288, 1967.

15. Roger, Fred L.: "Sequential Complexity and Motor Response Rates," *J. Exp. Psychol.; 74,* 199–202, 1967.

16. Swink, Joy, Trimbo, Don, and Noble, Merrill: "On the Length Difficulty Relation in Skill Performance," *J. Exp. Psychol.; 74,* 356–362, 1967.

Appendix A.

Six-Category Gross-Motor Test*

Averages, Scoring, Administrative
Procedures and Research Findings

*From Cratty, B. J.: Perceptual-Motor Behavior and Educational Processes. Springfield, Charles C Thomas Publisher, 1969.

TABLE 1: *Six-category gross-motor test*

ADMINISTRATION AND SCORING

LEVEL I—Test 1   *BODY PERCEPTION*

Equipment: 4 x 6 foot mat

Preparation: The child should be placed, standing on the floor, with his toes against the mid-point of the 4-foot edge of the mat. The tester should stand next to the child, with his feet on the floor.

General Consideration: The tester should describe and then demonstrate each movement, and then arise from the mat permitting the child to respond. The child should arise after each request and stand at the starting point described above. The child should be told ''thank you'' after attempting each movement.

Testing:

a. ''_____(name)_____, please lie down on the mat like this on your front or stomach.'' (Tester then lies on his stomach, his head away from the child, remains for two seconds, arises, and says . . .) ''Now try to do it too.'' Point is given if the child lies on his stomach regardless of whether or not head is turned away from or toward the tester.

b. ''_____(name)_____, now please lie down on the mat like this on your back.'' (Tester lies down slowly on his back, head away from the child, remains for two seconds, arises and then says, ''now try to do it too.''

c. ''_____(name)_____, now please lie down on the mat like this on your front or stomach, with your legs nearest me.'' (Tester assumes lying position, with his legs nearest the child, arises and then says . . .) ''Now try to do it too.'' The tester should then go to the far end of the 4-foot side of the mat, and face the child with the mat between them. Point is awarded only if feet are nearest the tester, and child is on his stomach.

d. ''_____(name)_____, now please lie down on the mat on your side, like this . . .'' (Tester lies down on his left side, feet toward the child, arises, and then says . . .) ''Now try to do it too.'' Point is awarded no matter which side the child chooses to lie upon, nor where the feet are relative to the tester.

e. The tester should then say, ''Now let me see you lie down on your left side.'' This should *not* be demonstrated. A 5th point is awarded in this category if the child correctly lies on his left side.

Scoring: One point is given for correctly executing each of the following requests. No points are deducted for a slowly executed response. Total of 5 points possible.

LEVEL I—Test 2   *GROSS AGILITY*

Equipment: 4 x 6 foot mat; stop-watch

Preparation: Child is asked to stand in the center of the mat, facing a 4-foot side and the tester. Tester should be 10 feet away. Then the child should be asked to lie down in the middle of the mat, his feet toward the tester.

Instructions: After the child is in the above position, the tester should say, ''I would like to see how fast you can stand up and face me.'' A stop-watch should be started as the child's head leaves the mat, and stopped as he has his knees straight as he assumes a standing position, facing the tester. If the child does not understand, the tester should demonstrate standing up rapidly.

Scoring: 1 point if the child turns to his stomach first and then arises in more than three seconds.

2 points if the child turns to his stomach first and arises under three seconds.

3 points if the child sits up, without turning over, and stands up without turning his back to the tester taking more than three seconds.

4 points if the child sits up, remains facing the tester when arising, and does so in two seconds.

5 points if the child sits up, remains facing the tester when arising, and does so under two seconds.

Note: A second hand on the standard watch may be used in lieu of a stop-watch. Maximum points possible, 5.

LEVEL 1—Test 3 *BALANCE*

Equipment: Stop-watch

Preparation: The tester should face the child on a level floor ten feet away.

Instructions: After getting the child in this position the tester should say . . . "I would like to see how long you can stand on one foot like this" . . . (the tester should demonstrate balancing on his left foot, using his arms to assist him and should then say . . ." Now you try it too." (Tester should demonstrate the held position for ten seconds.)

Scoring: 1 point if attempted and held for one second.

2 points if attempted and held from two to 4 seconds.

3 points if attempted and held from four to six seconds.

4 points if attempted and held over 6 seconds.

Second part: "Now let's see if you can balance on one foot with your arms folded, like this." (Tester should demonstrate by posturing on one foot with arms folded across his chest for ten seconds.)

Scoring: 5 points in this test if arm-folded balance is held from three to four seconds. Maximum 5 points possible.

Permit the child to remain balanced on both parts of this test for ten seconds, and then suggest that he stop. The scoring is not influenced by the foot he decides to balance upon, however, it should be the same foot throughout.

LEVEL I—Test 4 LOCOMOTOR AGILITY

Equipment: 4 x 6 foot mat

Preparation: Ask the child to stand on the floor, with his feet touching the mat in the middle of one of its 4-foot sides. The tester should place himself at the same end.

Instructions: After the child is in place, the tester says . . .

a. "_____(name)_____, let's see if you can crawl across the mat like this," (tester crawls on hands and knees in the correct pattern down the length of the mat away from the child, then toward the child, and then the tester says), "Now you try it too." One point scored if a correct cross-extension pattern is seen in the crawling movement.

b. "_____(name)_____, let's see now if you can walk down the mat like this," (tester walks down the mat away from the child and then says), "Now let's see if you can do it too." Additional point is scored if cross-extension pattern is seen in gait.

c. "_____(name)_____, now can you jump a cross the mat like this?" (tester takes three to four jumps across the mat, using both feet together and proper arm lift as he travels and then says), "Now you try too." One point is scored if the child leaves the ground two to three times during trip down the mat.

d. "_____(name)_____, now let's see you jump backwards down the mat like this." (tester jumps backwards toward the child and then says), "Now let me see you do it." A point is given if the child can jump backwards two to three times without falling down, proceeding down the mat. He is permitted to look behind himself when executing this test. Tester should return to the far end of the mat and await the child, stop him and prevent him from falling on the floor as he completes his trip.

e. "_____(name)_____, now let's see you hop down the mat on one foot like this," (tester demonstrates one foot hopping, using his left foot across the mat away from the child and then says), "Now let me see you do it." One additional point is scored if child is able to hop on one (either one) from two to three times down the mat.

Maximum 5 points possible.

LEVEL I—Test 5 *BALL THROWING*

Equipment: Rubber playground ball, 8 inches in diameter

Preparation: Ball is placed at the child's feet, tester faces the child, 15 feet away.

Testing: The child is asked to pick up the ball and throw it to the tester. The tester should say, "_____(name)_____, please pick up the ball and throw it to me." (The tester should then execute a proper one-handed overhand throwing movement.) And at the same time should say, "Like this." The ball is rolled back to the child, and he should be permitted five throws.

Scoring: 1 point is given if he pushes the ball with his hands or feet.
2 points are given if he throws the ball, either overhand or underhand using both arms at the same time.
3 points are given if the ball is thrown with one arm without any body shift into the throw.
4 points are given if the child throws with a weight shift forward of the body, without proper step on the opposite foot.
5 points are given if the child throws with a weight shift at the time the ball is released, and with a step with the opposite foot occurring at the same time.
Give the child the proper score based upon the habitual way he selected to throw the ball, *i.e.,* the manner in which he throws it three out of five times. Maximum 5 points possible.

LEVEL I—Test 6 *BALL TRACKING*

Equipment: $8\frac{1}{2}$ inch rubber, air-filled playground ball

Preparation: The child should face the tester 10 feet away. The tester should hold the ball.

Testing: The tester should then say, "Now I will bounce the ball to you. Try to catch it any way you can." (The tester then throws the ball, so that it bounces once before the child gets it. The ball should bounce, so that it comes chest high to the child. Two practice bounces are permitted to allow the child and tester to become oriented to the problem.) The tester should then say, "Now do you understand? Catch it any way you can, with one or two hands."

Five throws should then be made to the child, bouncing the ball once. The ball may be returned by the child, any way he sees fit. About 5 seconds should be permitted between throws.

Scoring: Score 1 point for each time the ball is caught and controlled by the child. Maximum 5 points possible.

LEVEL II—Test I *BODY PERCEPTION*

Equipment: 4 x 6 foot mat

Preparation: The child is asked to lie on his back in the center of the mat, with his feet pointed toward the 4 foot end; the tester should stand at this end.

Testing: The tester should say . . . _____(name)_____, now I am going to ask you to do certain things with your arms and legs, please try to do them as quickly and as accurately as you can. First close your eyes . . .'' Then the tester should say

1. ''Raise your left arm in the air.'' Then the tester should wait until the child makes a decision and moves. Then the tester says, ''Put your arm down now . . .''

2. The tester should then say, ''Raise your left leg up.'' The tester should wait until the leg is decided upon and moved and then say, ''Put your leg down now . . .''

3. The tester should then say, ''Raise your right arm in the air.'' The tester should wait until the child selects an arm and raises it and should then say, ''Put your arm down now.''

4. The tester should then say, ''Touch your left elbow with your right. ''After some movement is made, the tester should say, ''Now bring your hand down again.''

5. The tester should then say, ''Touch your right knee with your left hand.'' After these movements are completed, the tester should ask the child to open his eyes and come to his feet.

Scoring: One point is awarded for each correctly executed movement. No points are deducted for slowly executed movements. If in numbers 1 through 5, the movements are correct, but with wrong hand in every case, *i.e.* all movements backwards, a total of 3 points is awarded to the child for this test. Maximum of 5 points possible.

LEVEL II—Test 2 *GROSS AGILITY*

Equipment: 4 x 6 foot mat

Preparation: Child is placed in the center of the mat, standing and facing one of the 6-foot edges. The tester stands 10 feet away facing the child.

Tester: ''_____(name)_____, see if you can kneel down on one knee at a time, and then stand up on one leg at a time like this without touching anything.'' (The tester then executes a four count, one to the second, movement kneeling first on one knee, then on the second, then standing on the first foot and arising on the two feet . . . the tester says then, ''Do you understand? ''Would you like to see it again?'' If the child wished to see the movement again, the tester should do so . . . and after this second demonstration, the tester should then say, ''Now you try it too.''

Scoring: 1 point is awarded if the child uses his hands on his thighs *and* on the floor to assist him in descending and/or arising.

2 points are awarded if the child touches one or both hands to his thighs when ascending and descending, or if the child comes down to both knees at once, or gets to both feet at the same time.

3 points are awarded if the child uses one or both hands while getting up only, or if he falls to one knee while arising.

4 points are awarded if the child executes movement without the use of the hands, but there is general unsteadiness, *i.e.* extra steps taken as the child resumes his feet, etc.

5 points are awarded if the child executes movement perfectly with the hands at the sides, not assisting the movement, and with the feet coming down and up separately.

No points are deducted if the child comes up first with a different foot from the one kneeled upon. Maximum 5 points possible.

LEVEL II—Test 3 *BALANCE*

Equipment: stop-watch

Preparation: Place the child in the standing position, on a level floor and facing away from obstacles with the tester ten feet away.

Testing: After placing the subject in the position described above, the tester should say,
a. "I would like to see how long you can stand on one foot like this (the tester should fold his arms) with your arms folded and stand on one foot for ten seconds."
b. If the child can accomplish this for five seconds or more, the tester should say, "I would now like you to balance on one foot like this, with your arms at your sides, and your eyes closed."
c. If the child can accomplish this for five seconds or more, the tester should say, "I would like you to balance on one foot with your eyes closed and your arms folded like this." The tester should demonstrate with eyes closed, an arm-folded, one foot balance.
d. If the child can accomplish this for five seconds, the tester should say, "Now try to balance on one foot with your eyes closed, arms held at your sides, but using the other foot this time." The tester should be aware of the foot preferred by the child, and request that the opposite one be used.
e. If the child can accomplish this for five seconds, the tester should say, "Now try to balance on the same foot (non-preferred) with your arms folded and your eyes closed.

Scoring: One point is scored for each of the tests above completed successfully, *i.e.* held over five seconds. No points are given if the arms become unfolded, if they are required to be folded . . . nor if the child opens his eyes when they are required to be closed.

In each case the stop-watch should be started, or the second hand observed, as the foot leaves the ground, and stopped when it touches the next time. "Arms at your sides", means that the child can use the arms for maintaining his balance in any way that is helpful.

From ten to fifteen seconds rest should be permitted between trials. Maximum 5 points possible.

LEVEL II—Test 4 *LOCOMOTOR AGILITY*

Equipment: 4 x 6 foot mat laid out in 12 one-foot squares

Preparation: The child should face the tester at the far end of the middle of a 4-foot side. The tester should stand on the floor with his feet at the middle of the other end of the 4-foot side of the mat, facing the child.

Testing: With the child and tester in the above positions, the tester should say . . .
a. "Now let's see if you can jump down the mat like this." (The tester then jumps two feet at a time down the mat moving straight ahead, and jumping carefully in all six squares.) The tester should then say, "Now let's see you do it . . . be sure to jump in each square and move straight ahead."
b. After this is attempted, the tester should say, "Now let's see you jump back and forth (using only the unmarked squares so that he jumps forward with each jump) like this" . . . the tester should then say, "Now let's see you do it . . . be sure to jump only in the unmarked squares."

c. After this is attempted, the tester should say, "Now let's see you jump backwards down the mat like this." (The tester should jump directly backwards down the mat, using both feet, and landing in all six squares.) The tester should then say, "Now let's see you do it too . . . be sure to jump in all six squares." The child can be permitted to look backwards as he jumps.

d. After this is attempted, the tester should say, "Now let's see you hop down the mat like this." (The tester should then hop on the mat straight ahead, using all six squares.) The tester should then say, "Now let's see you do it. Jump in each square and move straight ahead."

e. After this is attempted, the tester should say, "Now let's see you hop down the mat like this." (The tester should then hop on one foot, hopping only in the unmarked squares, so that every hop moves him forward and from side to side.) The tester should then say, "Now let's see you do it too . . . be sure only to hop in the unmarked squares."

Scoring: One point is given for each successful trip, *i.e.* one with less than two errors in it. An error is scored when a foot(or feet) does not land in a square, when the second foot is touched, when hopping on one foot, or when an extra step is taken in a square. Maximum 5 points possible.

Ten to fifteen seconds rest should be permitted between trips. Either foot may be used for hopping, but the same foot must be used for each trip.

LEVEL II—Test 5 *BALL THROWING*

Equipment: Playground Ball 8' in diameter. 4' by 6' mat with target side up.

Preparation: The child should stand 15 feet away from the 4-foot end of the mat.

Testing: After the child has assumed the above position, the tester should stand next to him and throw the ball toward the mat's center on which is painted a 2 x 2 feet square "target"/This should be done three times . . . and the tester should then say, "I would like to take this ball and try to make it drop in the center of the mat . . . Do you understand?"

If the child is aware of the nature of the task he is permitted to throw, either overhand or underhand, with one or two hands, at the target . . . 5 times.

Scoring: 1 point is given if three attempts have hit the mat, but not the center target.
2 points are given if five attempts have hit the mat, but not the target.
3 points are given if two attempts have hit the target regardless where other throws have landed.
4 points are given if three attempts have hit the target, regardless where other throws have landed.
5 points are given if four or five throws land within the target.
The child receives *one* of the scores above *i.e.* highest score possible, 5 points.

LEVEL II—Test 6 *BALL TRACKING*

Equipment: Rubber softball hung on a string

Preparation: The tester should face the child about 2 feet away, he should ask the child to extend his arm at the shoulder, fist clenched. He should then suspend the ball on the 15-inch string so that it hangs, when motionless at the level of the child's chin (top of the ball just under the chin), and a distance away determined by the length of the child's arm plus the clenched fist.

The ball should then be suspended by the tester's left hand so that it hangs as described above. The ball should then be grasped with the tester's right hand, brought to a position which makes the string horizontal, and released so that it swings from the child's left to right in a vertical plane, parallel to the one in which the child is standing.

Testing: The tester should then permit the ball to swing back and forth in this manner 6 times and ask the child to watch it. The tester should then say, ''See this ball swing back and forth? See if you can touch it with one finger like this (the tester holds the ball motionless with one hand and uses the opposite index finger on the ball touching it quickly with the tip of the opposite index finger), as it passes by you.''

The tester should then hang the ball in front of the child and make sure that he starts his movement from his side, and that the touch is made directly in front of the child.

The tester should start the ball 5 times, allowing it to swing past the child 3 times after each release. As soon as the child touches it or attempts to, or the hand is extended, the ball comes back on it, and stops . . . the ball is stopped by the tester and started again.

Scoring: Score 1 point (maximum 5) for each time during each of the five sets of three swings each that the child is able to touch the ball. Make sure that no score is given if the ball touches the hand, *i.e.* as it swings back to the extended hand after a ''miss'' has occurred.

TABLE 2: *Average scores of normal children by age and sex on the six-category gross-motor test*

BOYS

	Age	Body Perception		Gross Agility		Balance		Locomotor Agility		Throwing		Tracking		Total Battery	
		M	σ	M	σ	M	σ	M	σ	M	σ	M	σ	M	σ
(20)*	4	4.83	2.85	8.83	1.26	5.67	1.94	3.33	1.00	2.00	0.00	2.22	1.81	26.94	4.05
(22)*	5	6.12	2.54	9.56	0.80	6.60	1.20	4.36	1.92	2.16	0.78	4.24	2.06	33.00	4.99
(21)*	6	8.35	1.88	9.79	0.66	7.90	1.09	7.03	1.40	3.38	1.32	6.90	1.47	43.34	3.61
(27)*	7	9.00	1.90	9.67	1.05	8.00	1.02	7.15	1.61	5.00	1.98	7.26	1.00	46.07	3.83
(20)*	8	8.90	1.82	9.71	1.07	8.38	0.99	7.76	1.19	6.67	2.12	7.76	0.92	49.19	5.41
(23)*	9	9.65	1.11	9.70	1.10	8.60	0.86	9.05	0.97	7.15	1.93	8.10	0.62	52.40	3.69
(17)*	10	8.81	3.05	9.52	2.13	9.19	0.73	9.29	0.76	7.86	1.58	7.86	1.04	52.52	5.10
(22)*	11	9.35	2.24	9.13	2.40	9.48	0.65	9.30	1.41	8.13	2.31	8.26	1.70	53.70	7.99

Based upon scores obtained from 172 boys.
*Number of children in each group.
M = Mean
σ = Standard deviation

TABLE 3: Average scores of normal children by age and sex on the six-category gross-motor test

GIRLS

Age		Body Perception		Gross Agility		Balance		Locomotor Agility		Throwing		Tracking		Total Battery	
		M	σ	M	σ	M	σ	M	σ	M	σ	M	σ	M	σ
(18)*	4	4.60	1.49	6.65	2.10	4.20	1.03	5.25	1.13	4.10	1.38	3.40	2.33	28.45	5.61
(24)*	5	6.45	2.77	8.64	1.77	5.64	1.61	6.32	1.74	3.14	1.32	5.64	2.85	36.27	8.71
(29)*	6	8.38	1.81	8.33	1.91	7.00	1.63	6.29	1.27	5.24	1.33	7.05	1.56	42.29	6.46
(28)*	7	9.30	1.43	8.70	1.60	8.26	1.58	7.18	1.59	7.15	1.63	8.26	1.45	48.85	5.58
(21)*	8	9.70	0.64	9.10	1.26	8.05	1.60	9.15	0.91	8.45	1.47	8.90	0.99	53.55	4.35
(20)*	9	9.48	1.06	9.70	0.58	9.17	1.00	8.65	1.09	8.17	1.24	9.48	0.58	54.74	2.40
(21)*	10	9.82	0.71	9.88	0.47	9.23	1.26	9.23	1.06	8.88	1.08	9.82	0.38	56.71	3.80
(22)*	11	9.68	1.05	9.88	0.43	9.24	0.91	9.24	0.86	9.04	0.87	9.76	0.58	54.76	9.62

Based upon scores obtained from 183 girls.
*Number of children in each group.
M = Mean
σ = Standard deviation

TABLE 4: *Six-category gross-motor test*

CORRELATION MATRIX

		1	2	3	4	5	6	7
Body Perception	1.							
Gross Agility	2.	.32						
Balance	3.	.53	.28					
Locomotor Agility	4.	.48	.35	.62				
Throwing	5.	.52	.21	.70	.57			
Tracking	6.	.54	.36	.72	.62	.72		
Total Battery Score	7.	.73	.48	.82	.75	.81	.84	

All correlations are positive.

TABLE 5: *Factor analysis, six-category gross-motor test battery**

FACTOR I Age and General Skill	Age .57; Balance .42; Locomotor Agility .32; Ball Throw .85
FACTOR II Balance and Body Agility	Balance (Level I) .96; Balance (Level II) .79; Agility (Level I) .94; Agility (Level II) .95
FACTOR III Ball Handling, General	Locomotor Agility (Level I) .50; Ball Throwing (Level I) .52; Ball Catching (Level II) .61.
FACTOR IV Body-Perception	Body Perception (Level I) .70; Body Perception (Level II) .81; Perception, Total Score .99
FACTOR V Hand-eye, Foot-eye Coordination	Gross Agility (Total Score) .54; Locomotor Agility (Level II) .31; Ball Tracking (Level I) .57; Ball Tracking (Total) .61; Total Battery Score .46.
FACTOR VI Balance and Tracking	Balance (Level II) .39; Balance (Total) .49; Ball Tracking (Total) .35.

*Six hundred and fifty childrens' scores utilized. Taken from correlation matrix in which 19 variables were compared, including tests and sub-test scores. The Pearson Produce-Moment formula was used as a graphic representation of the data revealed linearity. The data were then subjected to a minimum residual factor analysis, using a program designed by Comrey (FORTRAN IV Program, Dept. of Psychology, UCLA, 1964). This program performed a varimax rotation of the minimum residual matrix thus the varimax matrix was the final output. Only factor loadings exceeding .3 are listed.

14

TABLE 6: *Comparison of pre-and post-test means of 65 children with moderate motor problems, after participation for five months in a program of movement education.**

	Pre-test		Post-test		t
	M	σ	M	σ	
Body Image	8.11	2.08	8.09	2.08	.08
Gross Ability	8.07	1.92	8.65	1.84	2.49†
Balance	5.48	2.29	6.39	2.59	3.81*
Locomotor Ability	6.54	1.81	7.74	2.07	5.93†
Throwing	4.30	1.82	5.04	2.25	3.43†
Tracking	6.22	2.23	7.39	2.67	3.71†
Total Score	38.74	9.21	43.33	10.36	6.02†

† = Significant at the 1% level of confidence
* = Significant at the 5% level of confidence
*Mean age of the group was 8.92, SD 2.48, there were 57 boys, 8 girls.
M = Mean
σ = Standard deviation

Appendix B.

Drawing Tests

Test Procedures, Norms, Scoring,
Research Results

TABLE 7: *Geometric figure drawing and conglomerate tests*

ADMINISTRATIVE INSTRUCTIONS

Equipment and Facilities:

Small room with good lighting and limited distractions, *i.e.* no posters, pictures, or toys.

Table large enough for two, having a flat, *smooth* surface.

Two chairs, one of adjustable height for the child, and the other placed to the left of the child for the instructor.

Number 2 pencil without eraser is needed for the child.

Medium point, black ballpoint pens (*e.g.* Fisher Office Pen CR 64-39), are needed for the tester.

Blank sheet of paper (8 x 11) is to be used, *one* per child.

Standard Figure ditto for the child to copy.

Standard Drawing ditto (blank sheet of paper with standard drawing reversed (mirror-image) so the tester can trace from the other side). *One new ditto standard must be used for each test.*

Procedure:

Introduce yourself to the child. Then ask the child to be seated at the table. Adjust his chair so that he is in a good writing position, laterally and vertically. Place a blank sheet of paper in front of him and hand him the pencil he is to use.

The tester sits to the right of the child.

The test battery consists of two parts. The first contains five drawings. Each is to be drawn by the child on a separate sheet of paper, and each sheet of paper is held vertically by the tester as the child draws. The model is kept face down until time of use, when it is at that time placed flat in front of the child and to the top of the test sheet. The child copies the models which are to be shown in this order: CIRCLE, SQUARE, RECTANGLE, TRIANGLE, AND DIAMOND. When the child has completed each figure, the tester should mark the starting point (x), indicate the direction each line was drawn (with an arrow), and place in a separate pile face down. Directions to the child are simply: "I want you to copy this figure EXACTLY." This is stated for each figure before the child begins to draw.

When the child has finished the first part of the test, tell him: "We are now going to draw a series of figures."

The second portion of the test is made up of ten figures drawn in a series. (See sequence of figures for exact order.) Give the child one sheet of paper which is to be used horizontally. The tester obtains one standard drawing ditto for each child which is also to be placed horizontally for drawing (p. 198). The tester then draws figure one (the big square is 1). Now obtain the standard ditto and trace the second figure (the triangle in the left hand corner). Again place the standard in front of the child and to the top of the test sheet for the child to copy. Give him the same directions. When he has finished, number the starting point (this time with a 2).

This procedure is followed for all ten figures.

TABLE 8: *Sequence of figure drawing*

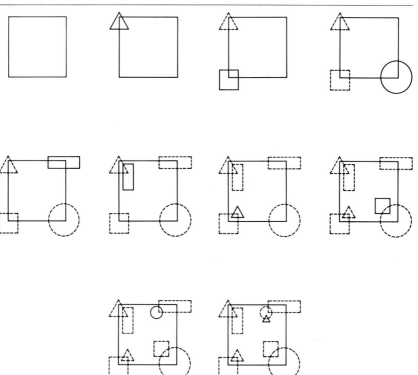

TABLE 9: *Conglomerate test*

MASTER TESTING SHEET

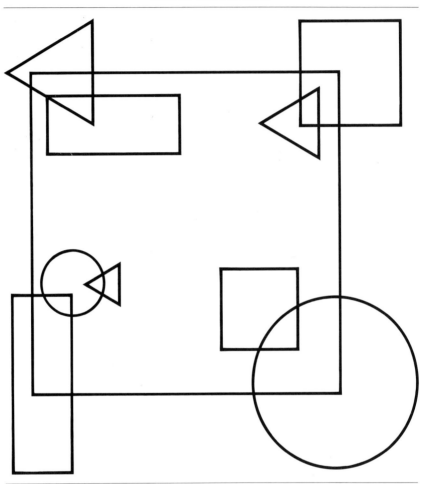

TABLE 10-A: *Geometric figure drawing test*

TEST SHEET #1

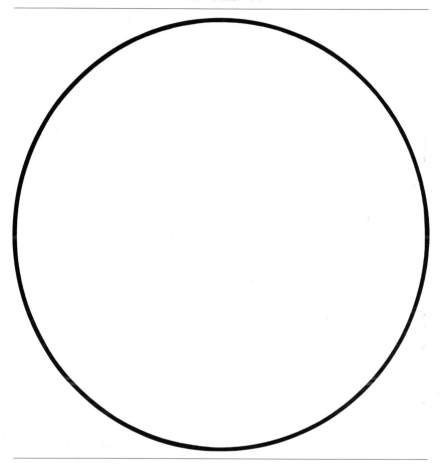

TABLE 10-B: *Geometric figure drawing test*

TEST SHEET #2

TABLE 10-C: *Geometric figure drawing test*

TEST SHEET #3

TABLE 10-D: *Geometric figure drawing test*

TEST SHEET #4

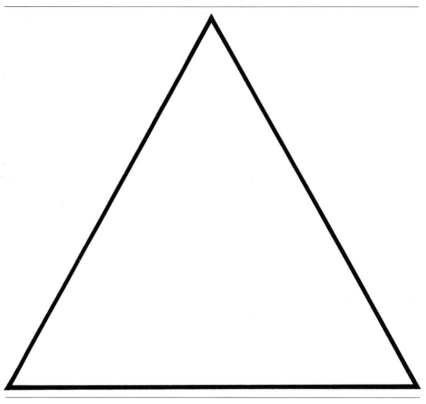

TABLE 10-E: *Geometric figure drawing test*

TEST SHEET #5

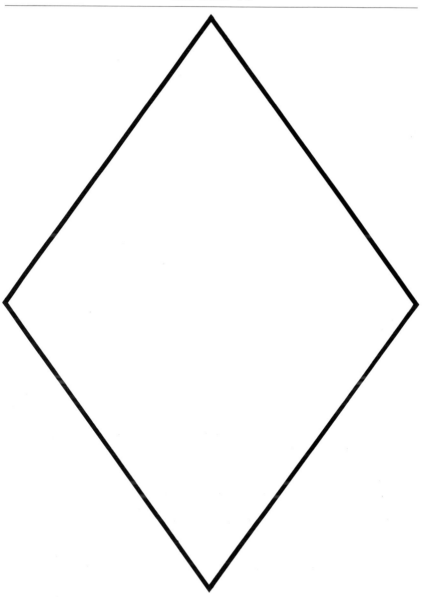

TABLE 11: *Scoring procedures, geometric figure drawing test*

Each Figure is scored separately; Two separate qualities are scored, Accuracy and Size.

ACCURACY: Each child's figure is compared to the norms on the following page, and a score is awarded each figure depending upon the norm figure, or 1, 2, or 3, to which it matches.

SIZE: Size is scored by superimposing each of the models on the corresponding figures drawn by the child. One point is scored if the child's figure is contained within the model. Two points are scored if the child's figure roughly corresponds in size to that of the model, while a score of 3 is awarded if the figure drawn by the child completely contains the model figure.

Mean of Inter-Tester Reliability = .92, based upon 40 children. Test-Re-Test reliability, based upon 40 children was as follows:

	Size	Accuracy
Circle	.95	.80
Square	.92	.78
Rectangle	.97	.82
Triangle	.95	.80
Diamond	.94	.83

TABLE 12: *Conglomerate test, scoring procedures*

ACCURACY: An accuracy score is obtained in this test by first comparing each of the figures drawn, and the first large square drawn to the scoring key on page 198, designed to assess accuracy of the individual geometric figure test. The final accuracy score on the conglomerate test is obtained by summing the accuracy scores obtained on each of the 10 figures within the final diagram and then dividing by 10.

LOCATION: A location score is obtained by scoring each of the figures drawn as either correctly placed (1) or incorrectly placed (0). To obtain a correct (1) score the smaller figure must be at the correct angle as well as at the correct location within the total diagram. Total location score possible is thus 10.

SIZE: Size is determined by superimposing the model on the child's drawing, figure by figure. If the child's figure is completely within the mode, score 1 point, if the child's drawing roughly coincides score a 2, and if the child's figure completely contains the model figure, score a 3.

Test Re-Test Reliabilities, based upon 30 children's drawings were: Size .89, Location .90 and Accuracy .81.

Inter-Observer (Scorer) reliabilities were: Size .92, Location .95 and Accuracy .82.

TABLE 13: *Geometric figure drawing test*

ACCURACY SCORING CHART

TABLE 14: *Average scores, by age, geometric figure drawing test*

Age	Circle				Square				Rectangle				Triangle				Diamond			
	Size		Accuracy		Size		Accuracy		Size		Accuracy		Size		Accuracy		Size		Accuracy	
	M	σ	M	σ	M	σ	M	σ	M	σ	M	σ	M	σ	M	σ	M	σ	M	σ
5 (53)*	1.0	.5	1.9	.8	1.7	.9	1.8	.5	1.4	.8	1.8	.5	1.7	.9	1.7	.6	1.4	.7	1.7	.6
6 (65)*	1.5	.7	2.0	.7	1.9	.9	2.0	.5	1.7	.9	1.8	.4	1.7	.9	2.0	.6	1.6	.9	1.7	.7
7 (47)*	1.5	.7	2.2	.7	1.5	.8	2.3	.5	1.6	.9	2.2	.5	1.6	.8	2.5	.6	1.4	.8	2.1	.6

*Number of children in each age group.

M = Mean

σ = Standard deviation

TABLE 15: *Average scores for 165 normal children, by age, in the conglomerate figure test*

AGE		Size		Accuracy		Location	
		M	σ	M	σ	M	σ
(53)*	5	2.1	.9	1.1	.4	3.3	3.0
(65)*	6	2.1	1.0	1.8	.5	6.9	2.9
(47)*	7	1.6	.8	2.1	.4	9.0	1.9

*Number of children in each age group.
M = Mean
σ = Standard deviation

TABLE 16

	Intercorrelations Between Size and Accuracy of Childrens Drawings of Geometric Figures, Listed by Age*					
	Age	Circle	Square	Rectangle	Triangle	Diamond
(53)*	5	.03	.27	.10	.23	.02
(65)*	6	.08	.00	.01	.01	.07
(47)*	7	.12	.22	.02	.23	.06

All correlations are positive.
*Number of children in each group.

	Intercorrelations Between Size, Accuracy and Location Scores, Obtained from 165 Normal Children in the Conglomerate Figure Drawing Test		
AGE	Size-Accuracy	Accuracy-Location	Location-Size
5	.20	.45	.09
6	.11	.49	.04
7	.19	.15	.16

*based upon scores of 165 normal children.

TABLE 17: *Mean scores of conglomerate figure drawing test by 65 children participating in a motor development program, pre-and post-test comparisons.**

	Pre-Test		Post-Test		t
	M	σ	M	σ	
Size	1.62	0.61	1.82	0.57	2.04
Accuracy	9.51	5.26	9.84	5.18	1.03
Location	5.29	3.47	7.04	3.35	5.68

*Mean age of the group was 8.92 SD 2.48, 57 boys, and 8 girls.

Appendix C.

Games Choice Test, Self-Opinion Test, and Physical Fitness Test

TABLE 18: *Revised Sutton-Smith games choice test*

ADMINISTRATION AND SCORING PROCEDURES

Preparation: The child should be seated to the right of the tester at the table.

General consideration: The tester should ask the question, attempting to omit in his voice inflections that may influence the child's responses. In order to establish rapport with the child the tester should ask the child whether or not he has brothers and/or sisters, and their ages. He should record these responses.

Testing:

,, ____(name)____, I'm going to ask you about some games. After I say the game, either you tell me 'yes' if you like to play that game, or you tell me 'no' if you do not like to play that game, or you tell me 'I don't know' if you don't know that game." (Tester then begins with the first question). "Do you like to play ____(the game)____?" (Tester waits for the child to respond and then proceeds to the next game).

Scoring:

a. General: If the child says "yes", then the tester should mark "Y" to the left of that game. If the child says "no" or "I don't know", then the tester should mark "N" to the left of that game.

b. Specific: Each game on the list has been given a weighted score by Sutton and Smith. Minimum score is 1 point, maximum score is 3 points. The weights of the "yes" responses in the boy's game category are totaled. Then the weights of the "yes" responses in the girls' game category are totaled separately. The minimum total for each category is zero points (if the child responded "no" to all the games in that category), and the maximum total for each category is 50 points (if the child responded "yes" to all the games in that category).

TABLE 19: *Revised Sutton-Smith, game choice list*

3 M	1.	Soldiers	3 M	20.	Toy Trains
3 F	2.	House	3 M	21.	Darts
2 F	3.	Doctors	3 F	22.	Dance
1 M	4.	Cowboys	3 M	23.	Wrestling
3 M	5.	Hunting	3 F	24.	Sewing
2 M	6.	Cars	3 F	25.	See Saw
3 M	7.	Cops and Robbers	3 M	26.	Football
1 M	8.	Wall Dodgeball	3 F	27.	Dolls
2 M	9.	Marbles	3 M	28.	Bows and Arrows
3 F	10.	Hopscotch	3 M	29.	Shooting
3 M	11.	Use Tools	3 F	30.	Jacks
3 F	12.	Jump Rope	3 M	31.	Make Model Airplanes
3 M	13.	Boxing	3 F	32.	Drop the Handkerchief
1 M	14.	Bowling	3 F	33.	Store
2 M	15.	Bandits	3 F	34.	Farmer in the Dell
3 M	16.	Spaceman	3 F	35.	Ring Around the Rosy
3 F	17.	London Bridge	3 F	36.	Mother May I?
3 F	18.	Cooking	3 F	37.	Musical Chairs
2 M	19.	Build Forts			

TOTAL SCORES

boys' game score

girls' game score

Total Possible ___50___

Total Possible ___50___

With permission of Dr. Brian Sutton-Smith

TABLE 20: *Average scores, by sex and age, for the games-choice test*

GIRLS' MEAN SCORES

	Age	Weighted Scores				Number of Choices			
		Boys' Games		Girls' Games		Boys' Games		Girls' Games	
		M	σ	M	σ	M	σ	M	σ
(71)*	7	14.48	12.08	28.32	4.12	06.51	4.73	08.83	1.08
(71)*	8	8.97	7.02	25.53	6.13	4.14	2.92	7.13	1.72
(90)*	9	9.60	15.79	19.16	7.57	3.96	3.28	5.26	2.24
(70)*	10	7.60	8.01	15.00	6.53	3.16	2.68	4.46	1.86

*Number of children in each group.

TABLE 21: *Average scores, by sex and age, for the games-choice test*

BOYS' MEAN SCORES

| Age | | Weighted Scores | | | | Number of Choices | | | |
| | | Boys' Games | | Girls' Games | | Boys' Games | | Girls' Games | |
		M	σ	M	σ	M	σ	M	σ
(63)*	7	45.33	5.79	14.33	0.74	18.15	8.4	7.54	3.72
(74)*	8	36.82	10.53	9.57	6.88	15.10	7.98	6.32	4.01
(82)*	9	26.64	12.09	3.55	4.09	10.27	4.63	3.25	7.13
(83)*	10	20.77	10.44	1.71	2.59	8.08	4.26	2.96	1.01

*Number of children in each group.

TABLE 22: *Average scores, by sex, for the revised games—choice test by children in a program for the remediation of moderate motor problems.*

BOYS' MEAN SCORES

| | Weighted Scores | | | | Number of Games | | | |
| | Boys' Games | | Girls' Games | | Boys' Games | | Girls' Games | |
	M	σ	M	σ	M	σ	M	σ
(57)*	29.00	14.00	18.53	15.00	12.00	5.12	6.64	5.60

GIRLS' MEAN SCORES

| | Weighted Scores | | | | Number of Games | | | |
| | Boys' Games | | Girls Games | | Boys' Games | | Girls' Games | |
	M	σ	M	σ	M	σ	M	σ
(8)*	8.57	3.99	22.86	12.31	4.00	1.31	7.71	4.23

*Number of children in each group.
18.9 years (SD 2.48)

TABLE 23: *Self-opinion test*

TESTING AND SCORING PROCEDURES

Preparation: The child should be seated to the right of the tester at a table.

General considerations: The tester should begin by asking the child simple questions, in order to establish rapport. The tester should then begin to ask the questions on the following page.

Testing:

''____(name)____, where do you go to school?'' (The tester listens to the response, but does not record it). ''What grade are you in?'' (The tester listens to the response, but does not record it). ''Are you good at making things with your hands?'' (The tester listens to the response, and records to the right of the question either ''Y'' for a ''yes'' response or ''N'' for a ''no'' response. The tester then proceeds to the next question).

Scoring:

The responses are scored according to the key. Responses that do not correspond to the key are ''negative'' responses, indicating a low self-concept on a given response. These ''negative'' responses are totaled.

TABLE 24: *Self-opinion test*

QUESTIONS AND KEYS

1. Are you good at making things with your hands?	(17 Per cent)* __Y__ (28 Per cent)[+]
2. Can you draw well?	(18 Per cent)* __Y__ (36 Per cent)
3. Are you strong?	(22 Per cent) __Y__ (25 Per cent)
4. Do you like the way you look?	(13 Per cent) __Y__ (26 Per cent)
5. Do your friends make fun of you?	(40 Per cent) __N__ (45 Per cent)
6. Are you handsome/pretty?	(18 Per cent) __Y__ (28 Per cent)
7. Do you have trouble making friends?	(33 Per cent) __N__ (38 Per cent)
8. Do you like school?	(23 Per cent) __Y__ (16 Per cent)
9. Do you wish you were different?	(33 Per cent) __N__ (34 Per cent)
10. Are you sad most of the time?	(17 Per cent) __N__ (20 Per cent)
11. Are you the last to be chosen in games?	(39 Per cent) __N__ (50 Per cent)
12. Do girls like you?	(30 Per cent) __Y__ (44 Per cent)
13. Are you a good leader in games and sports?	(34 Per cent) __Y__ (30 Per cent)
14. Are you clumsy?	(23 Per cent) __N__ (30 Per cent)
15. In games do you watch instead of play?	(28 Per cent) __N__ (31 Per cent)
16. Do boys like you?	(13 Per cent) __Y__ (17 Per cent)
17. Are you happy most of the time?	(11 Per cent) __Y__ (6 Per cent)
18. Do you have nice hair?	(16 Per cent) __Y__ (14 Per cent)
19. Do you play with younger children a lot?	(25 Per cent) __N__ (38 Per cent)
20. Is reading easy for you?	(23 Per cent) __Y__ (23 Per cent)

*Per cent of 65 children participating in a program for the remediation of motor problems giving *negative* responses to each question. Average age 8.9 years, (SD 2.48), 57 boys, 8 girls.

[+] Per cent of *Negative* responses on the scale by the same group *after* a program of perceptual-motor education.

With permission of Dr. Ellen Piers

TABLE 25: *Physical fitness tests*

ADMINISTRATION AND SCORING PROCEDURES

General consideration: The tester should describe each movement, and permit the child to respond. The child should arise after each request.

Testing:
a. Push-Ups: The tester should place himself on the mat in a front-lying position: feet together, legs rigid; hands shoulder width apart. He should bend his arms at the elbows, lowering his chest to the mat, and then push on the mat with his hands to finish the movement. He should repeat this movement twice, and say, "Now you try it as many times as you can in twenty seconds." The tester should note whether or not the child's back is straight in recording the number of push-ups.

b. Sit-Ups: The tester should position himself on the mat in a back-lying position, with the soles of his feet on the mat at hip width and with his legs bent at the knees. He should then lie back on the mat and clasp both hands behind his neck. He should attempt to sit up without moving his legs, and then lower his back again to the mat. He should repeat this movement twice, and say, "Now you try it as many times as you can in twenty seconds." When the child seats himself on the mat in a back-lying position, with the soles of his feet on the mat at hip width and with his legs bent at the knees, the tester should hold the child's ankles. The tester should record the number of sit-ups done by the child without moving his legs.

c. Pull-Ups: The tester tells the child to lie on his back on the mat. The tester stands over the child, facing the child, with his feet spread on both sides of the child. The tester grasps the bar with both hands held at the middle of the bar, held at the child's arms length. "Now I want you to grab both ends of the bar." When the child obeys, the tester says, "Now without moving your heels and keeping your body straight, I want you to pull yourself up to the bar using only your arms so that your chin touches the bar. Do it as many times as you can in twenty seconds." The number of pull-ups done by using only the arms, and not moving the heels and keeping the body straight, are recorded.

d. Reverse Sit-Ups: The tester should position himself on the mat on his stomach, with his arms stretched perpendicularly from his trunk and with his legs straight back. He should then raise his upper body off the mat by tightening his hips and his lower back, and by keeping his arms and legs rigid. The tester should say, "Now you try it for as long as you can in twenty seconds. The number of seconds in which the child is able to keep his upper body off the mat by tightening his hips and lower back, and by keeping his arms and legs rigid, should be recorded to a maximum of twenty seconds.

TABLE 26: *Comparison of pre- and post-fitness scores by 65 children taking part in a five-month program designed to remediate their moderate motor problems.**

	Pre-Test		Post-Test		
	M	σ	M	σ	t
PUSH-UPS	7.24	4.11	9.33	3.32	4.19
SIT-UPS	4.78	3.59	6.37	3.51	4.04
PULL-UPS	3.11	3.29	5.80	3.90	4.86
REVERSE SIT-UPS	14.37	6.71	17.00	4.73	2.93

*Average age 8.9 years, SD 2.48, 57 boys and 8 girls.

Index

217

DATE DUE